Contents

Foreword

We live in a business age without precedent: where there exist greater opportunities than ever for people – young and old – to devise and start a venture and prove a success on their own terms.

Though previous generations have lionised successful business people, it wasn't the nature of their entrepreneurial skill, nor the promise of their idea, which gained them admiration, rather the end (often mass-produced) result. Henry Ford was admired for his savvy only when America's roads were crammed with Model Ts; yet today economists and business gurus focus on the faith that he had in his concept, and the dogged determination which brought his dreams to realisation on a Detroit production line.

Success remains the ultimate yardstick for whether an entrepreneur and his or her idea should be respected. However, the Internet has prompted a profound acceleration in the development, growth, success – and, indeed, failure – of companies and concepts: a business model that once would have taken decades to develop, today can bear fruit in a matter of hours; an ill-thought-out merger is now exposed as flawed within weeks.

This is due to the speed at which a business concept can be devised and implemented online (we are dispensing with the need for tea-slurping builders or rosy-cheeked mayors to snip ribbons!), the success of targeted digital marketing in funnelling millions of potential customers towards a new concept, but also the proliferation and democratisation of information that allows the consumer to do their research and make an informed decision.

The past decade has seen investors and venture capitalists (VCs) buying into the potential of a digital concept immediately after it has come to market – and, on occasion, even before a site has launched.

In short, while we still respect the current-day Henry Fords, who have had their mettle tested and have been proven winners, we have also come to admire the people who come up with the big ideas. The Internet Age has prompted us to respect innovation – more so than in previous decades – because it has allowed us to witness the development of a service or concept first-hand, even if the first dot.com crash should also have taught us that substance ultimately remains more important than style.

It could be argued that my current media position as a household name when it comes to business is, in part, a consequence of this modern preoccupation with the innovative entrepreneur, and the accessibility of information that the Internet offers.

My business, Pall-Ex, provided a rather revolutionary solution for the organised distribution of palletised freight, and has a formula that has proved a success. Pall-Ex continues to embrace the digital age, incorporating the Internet within our broader business model. Over the past few years we have introduced TWINE, a revolutionary IT management system that helps our members and customers to manage consignments in real time, as well as benefit from a host of back office functions including finance, HR, warehouse and CRM solutions. We have also developed a bespoke content management system called Digihub, as well as introduced digital signature capture and other ways of making proof of delivery as efficient as possible. Each of these innovations is helping to produce real cost savings and bring new business to our members.

I am passionate about my sector, and the fact that haulage provides, in effect, the arteries of British business. However, I concede that this is not a sector of interest to all, nor is it easily understandable to the uninitiated. Watching the traffic to the Pall-Ex website after my first appearance on BBC's *Dragons' Den* was interesting: most people went to the front page of www.pallex.co.uk, had a look around at this company in an unfamiliar industry, and left shortly afterwards, but thousands actually stayed on the site for a while, clearly interested in finding out about what I did for a living, and using the site as a way to get their heads around it. I accept that as a woman in a male-dominated industry I am perhaps an interesting anomaly, but I would strongly argue that I would not be as interesting to the general public had the Digital Age not made heroes (and heroines!) out of innovative entrepreneurs and provided consumers with the tools to inform themselves.

The capitalist system is predicated upon the belief that anyone can make it, and that there is some magical cosmic balance which ensures that hard work guarantees success. This, as all entrepreneurs will tell you, is flawed logic. The only certainty in the business world is that doing absolutely no work will directly result in no success! Of the individuals who will try to set up a business this year, a large proportion will fail. It's that yardstick again.

However, I passionately believe that, in spite of recession – and often as a result of it – there are more opportunities than ever before for ambitious sorts. There has never been a better time to put everything on the line and chase entrepreneurial success. If you have a good idea, you have done your research and know that there is either a gap in the market or a whole new market to be created, then go for it. However, do so with an awareness of how the Internet can help or hinder the development and implementation of your idea.

Like me, Kate is a woman in an industry better known for its male heroes, and I suspect that – like me – she has, on occasion, used this fact to her advantage. Her distinctness has provided her with a chance to be circumspect, and I hope that her take on things, as outlined in this book, will help a new generation get to grips with how to successfully use the Internet to fulfil their ambitions.

Good luck!
Hilary Devey
Entrepreneur, TV Dragon, and founder of European palletised freight distribution network, Pall-Ex.

About the author

A reporter and journalist, Kate Russell started writing about technology, gaming and the Internet in 1995 and now appears weekly on the BBC's flagship technology programme, *Click*, as well as being a regular on the sofa at ITV's *Daybreak*. She has become known as an Internet expert, invited to comment on TV and radio shows of all types, as well as speaking at technology events around the world and lecturing at schools and universities in the UK. She is one of the pioneering 'digital migrants'. Her online presence predates Facebook and she was born before the first popular videogame, *Pong*, was released (but only just!). She writes technology columns for *National Geographic Traveller* magazine and *Web User* magazine in addition to blogging regularly at WorkingTheCloud.biz and other online destinations. She is also very active on the social web and was once described by the BBC's house magazine *Ariel* as a member of the 'twitterati'. You can find her on Twitter at @KateRussell, where she is normally very happy to interact with readers and viewers, offering advice and finding online tools for those with a particular request. She also posts quite a few pictures of her cats. Once you've finished reading this book, the 'Working the Cloud' app will continue to build

Reading Borough Libraries
0118 901 5950

Self Service Receipt for Borrowing

Name: 24126001225858

Title: Working the cloud : making the Internet work for you & your business

Item: 34126010900861

Due Back: Borrow successful

Title: Sams teach yourself Unreal engine 4 game development in 24 hours

Item: 34126011195198

Due Back: Borrow successful

Title: The devil and Sherlock Holmes : tales of murder, madness and obsession

Item: 34126010431032

Due Back: Borrow successful

Total Borrowing: 0
22/01/2022 14:20:05

Thank you for using the library.

For renewals visit
www.reading.gov.uk/libraries

into the ultimate collection of online tips, tricks and resources for small businesses and entrepreneurs, with regular updates and special features. To access more incredible interviews, reviews, guides and suggestions from Kate, make sure to download it free for Android and Apple devices.

Introduction

Introducing the cloud

Running a business has always been tough, but never more so than in the last five years. When the financial crisis hit home in 2008, Britain suffered one of the longest and deepest recessions of any major economy. Businesses were brought to their knees, with over 300,000 shutting down in 2008, and almost half a million going the same way the following year, leaving more than a million people jobless. In the face of rising costs and shrinking opportunities, no business, large or small, remains safe from the snapping jaws of recession. Whether you are a butcher, baker or microchip-maker, cutting costs and reaching a larger, more targeted audience will go a long way towards keeping you afloat. But that doesn't mean that you have to scale up production and blow loads of cash that you don't have on a flashy marketing campaign. I have spent the last nine years reporting on developments on the World Wide Web for the BBC and other broadcasters, online and print publications. If you think the financial geography of the world has changed in that time, the landscape of the Internet has changed even more – and when used correctly, it could prove to be the greatest asset in your economic crisis survival kit.

For many people a computer is all but invisible (until it stops working). It's something they use every day to complete mundane but essential tasks connected to running a business: invoicing, spreadsheets, email and maybe some basic research if they can filter out the noise that's returned in the average web search. This is especially true if you come from the same generation as I do: *digital migrants*. We weren't born with a silver mouse wired up to our umbilical cord. We had to learn things the hard way when the desktop computer really was a temperamental beast, little understood and to be feared and revered. I remember the first terminal I used in an office – it had a black screen with green text and ran on an undecipherable platform called UNIX that was talked about in hushed tones by serious-looking huddles of network engineers.

But now computers and smartphones are more powerful and easier to use than ever before. The processor running your average smartphone packs more digital punch than those used to put man on the moon. Over 2.2 billion people are connected to the Internet today, and that figure is set to explode as mobile Internet takes over. Ten years ago there were just 700 million mobile devices; today there are already nearly 5 billion, and some manufacturers are predicting that the figure will rise to a jaw-dropping 50 billion by 2020 – that's one heck of a lot of ways to connect to the Internet, and there is no longer any point in denying that the Internet is where it's at these days. Because of this accessibility there is an ever-expanding population choosing to work completely 'in the cloud'. In this context the term 'cloud' broadly just means the Internet. Someone who is 'working in the cloud' is accessing documents, files and information through services and applications hosted somewhere on the Internet rather than saved on the computer sitting under their desk. Things stored 'in the cloud' are accessible through an Internet browser, or maybe a dedicated application that you can download to your mobile or desktop device. This means that you can set up office pretty much anywhere you can find an Internet connection, which makes for a very flexible business model.

Even if you don't want to up sticks and move your digital life entirely onto the Internet, it's also awash with useful and ingenious software packages that you can download to make your life easier, cheaper and faster, or can use as an alternative to expensive commercial products that can drain hundreds of pounds you can't afford out of your start-up funds. So what kind of things are we talking about? And should you keep reading if you don't do any business at all online? The answer to that question is a resounding 'yes'.

If you're not online at all you are missing a serious trick. We used to reach for the *Yellow Pages* or *Thompson Local* when we wanted to find a nearby trader, but now most people just head for Google.com. Studies have shown that 85% of consumers have used an Internet search engine to find a local business, and 16% of them do so every week. If you have products to sell there is an even bigger opportunity because the buyer-to-seller ratio is more favourable than on the high street. Over 70% of Brits shop online, while only 14% of small businesses sell their goods online. Who wouldn't like to be operating in a less competitive market? There is also a growing trend for consumers to browse for a product on the high street before researching online to see if they can find it any cheaper. Smartphone apps let shoppers do this while they are still standing in the aisle, even scanning a barcode with their phone and being directed to outlets close by that are offering a better price. There is nowhere to hide on the Internet, it seems. All the power is in the hands of the connected consumer, literally, and while this might not seem very fair on the high street, there are ways that you can turn it to your advantage, even if you're one of those hard-done-by retailers struggling to cover your overheads. You might even be thinking about setting up an online shop, perhaps part time at first alongside your day job – for example, selling imported T-shirts or your own handmade jewellery. I'll be covering all this and more throughout the next 10 chapters.

And then there is the social web. The rise and rise of social media has changed the online dynamic in ways that no one could have predicted even as little as a decade ago. Now anyone can make and publish content – in text, images, video or audio – and have it connect them organically with a potentially huge audience if they get it right. If you're looking for more customers it has to be the most obvious place to go first. More than 60% of adults now use social media, so if you can find them you can start talking to them, building trust and recognition through finding, sharing and even creating content that they will find useful. If they like you, they will invite you into their own closed network, where you can talk to them directly about your business and what it could offer them. As well as building customer loyalty, this online relationship might lead to customers sharing your offers and promotions with their own circle of friends, and your reputation will blossom inside their network of contacts too.

Competition and customers aside, though, there is also a wealth of resources online to help you run the nuts and bolts of your business.

From entire management suites to simple tools to perform a specific function, I'm going to show you that the 'cloud' is bursting at the seams with websites and apps that will revolutionise the way you do business. If you don't have time to keep an eye on an important parcel delivery because you're up to your neck in accounting, I'll show you how to get Twitter to track the delivery for you, reporting back at every stage of the package's journey until it is safely in your hands. But why are you so busy with the accounts anyway? There are some great online finance and management tools to help you automate your administration and work more efficiently so that you can spend more time drumming up new business (or enjoying the profits). And if you can't face another long drive across town for a meeting with clients or colleagues, I'll show you ways to turn your computer into a virtual task room, fully equipped with all the communication and presentation aids you'll need and stuffed to the rafters with team creative tools to help get the ideas flowing. And to top up your turnover health, I'll show you how to get noticed online – rising through the search results when people look for the services you offer, and even getting complete strangers to work as evangelists on your behalf, promoting your business through sharing and recommending your content to local groups of interested people.

You might think you're getting along quite nicely without using the Internet very much, but I urge you to reconsider and pick up this book anyway. Within each chapter there is an interview with a business leader and inspiring entrepreneur, and without fail each one agreed that it is essential for a successful small business to be on the Internet these days. So, let me show you how to turn the Internet into your friend and business partner in *Working the Cloud*, an essential handbook for anyone who wants to do business better, cheaper, faster and more profitably using mostly free stuff that you can find online.

Note: The other thing that is true of the Internet is that it is always changing. Like shifting sands of silicon, the online landscape is in constant flux, so I have tried to base my advice in these chapters on the sturdy foundations of basic principles, backed up by a selection of websites and tools that are current and relevant while I write. Because I have been watching this space closely for almost a decade, I believe the majority of these resources will still be current when you pick up this book to read it in a few months' time. What I can't do, though, is predict any new technologies that might come along and disrupt the market after we go to print. For updates and news related to the content in this book, including tips and reviews of new and ground-breaking services that spring up, please join me at WorkingTheCloud.biz. You can also download the free WorkingTheCloud smartphone app, which delivers full video interviews with the inspirational business leaders and entrepreneurs whom you'll find profiled within each chapter.

Chapter 1

Taming the cloud

Begin your journey to take control of the Internet and all it has to offer

Every journey begins with one step; and step one is to get yourself online so that people can find your business and you can start building relationships and customer loyalty, as well as expanding your horizons to new potential markets. In this chapter we'll be covering the basics, the stuff you really *have* to do if you want to keep up with the competition. I want you to be bold in your ambitions, even if you feel that you have limited technical experience. Every website and resource recommended in these pages is totally manageable by a technology novice; it might take you a few minutes to step through written instructions or follow the on-screen prompts, but as long as you know how to turn on your computer and connect it to the Internet to browse websites and send or receive emails, you should be just fine. In this chapter we'll be covering the following areas:

- establishing your presence on the essential web
- registering and personalising the 'Big Four' social sites: Facebook, Twitter, LinkedIn and Google Plus
- what to do if someone is using your identity online
- interview with Seth Casteel, whose business went global after his photos of underwater dogs went viral
- how and why to share photos and images online
- general information and resources for all small businesses and start-ups

- free forms, advice and helpful communities for small businesses and entrepreneurs.

YOUR PLACE IN THE CLOUD

Identifying and securing your essential online real estate

The first thing you need to do is find your identity on the Internet. Google estimates there are about 5 million terabytes of data on the web – it would take more than a billion DVDs to store it all – so we must think carefully about where to be seen and how you want people to perceive you. Throughout these chapters I will be showing you what you can do with your identity once you've secured it, but for now we're just going to get you registered with the essential services so that they are ready for you once you start using them. If you've never really used the Internet for business you might think the list is a little excessive, but try to think of it as a new school blazer at the beginning of term. What was it your parents said? "You'll grow into it." And you did. It's the same deal with your Internet education. You'll grow into the websites and networks we're going to be snagging now. They're where you will meet the world online, in whatever capacity suits your particular business now or down the line a little. You might not think an online presence is relevant to you if you run a high street shop or family plumbing business, but, as I mentioned earlier, most people now use the Internet to search for local businesses, and those figures will only increase as broadband and mobile Internet penetration grows. There are a phenomenal number of places where you can exist online, from mainstream social platforms that you might have heard of to obscure specialist networks and blogging platforms. But, before you panic, you don't need to own all of them, and even if you do want to, there are tools that you can use to automate the process, selecting only those online properties most relevant to you.

knowem.com

KnowEm is a web service that lets you search for a name on over 600 social networks, 150 domain names and the entire US Trademark Database. It's completely free to use if you just want to explore the social, domain names and trademarks tabs separately, clicking the available links to register with those websites individually. You don't even need to register, though there is a range of premium options if you want the website to set up the profiles for you, saving a lot of time.

TIP

If you're just starting out in business you have the rare opportunity to take your social media identity into consideration when choosing a company name. A quick search will show you what's available. If this includes Facebook, Twitter and the appropriate top-level domain name – such as .com or .co.uk – you should grab this online real estate and start designing your business card.

namechk.com

Another option is NameChk. It's incredibly easy to use – just type in the desired name and click the links to register it. The database isn't as extensive as KnowEm (but do you really need 600 social options?) and it doesn't search domain names and US trademarks. But there is a free mobile app for Apple devices, so you can check all the most important websites the moment a name occurs to you.

about.me

As you register your presence your business card could start to look quite messy, so simplify things with about.me, which provides an online 'landing page', to house all of your virtual properties from one simple web address – for example about.me/WorkingTheCloud. This is a lot easier to print on a business card, and you can fully customise the way your page looks, adding text plus a background and profile picture, which in the case of a brand could be a logo. You can add all the popular social links with a few clicks, as the app will jump straight to an authorisation page if you're already logged in to those networks. Services that aren't covered by buttons can be included as web addresses. You can even activate your free email account and use the simple browser-based interface to handle your business correspondence with an easy-to-remember email address, like WorkingTheCloud@ about.me.

> **TIP**
>
> *Registering your name on a website will prevent other people from taking over the identity and confusing the brand message that your customers see online. Even if you never plan on posting anything to that platform, just grab the ID anyway and make sure that you include a link to your active online locations.*

SAY 'HELLO' TO THE CROWD

Getting social with your customers online

So, KnowEm searches through more than 600 'popular' social platforms – and that's a ridiculous number, right? First, I would argue the use of the term 'popular'. There are specialist platforms that are popular among their communities, but that doesn't mean that you need to secure your identity on 'Train Spotters United' if your business is about making fairy cakes (although that could be a missed opportunity, as I can imagine train spotters getting quite peckish when they're out by the train tracks). We'll be looking at the specialist networks later in this book to discover which ones are right for your business, but for now the number of 'essential' networks that you need to secure is a lot more manageable.

www.facebook.com

Social media is now the number one online activity – yes, it even overtook watching porn a few years ago – so the first place where you should expect to encounter your customers is on the social web. Arguably the single most important flag to capture is a Facebook brand page. With over a billion active monthly users spending over seven hours a month on the site, it's an unprecedented opportunity to talk directly to a community. People like to '*like*' stuff on Facebook, and if you can persuade them to give your page the thumbs up, they will be alerted in their daily news feed if you have any offers or promotions to run in the future. That's basically free, direct marketing, only they have invited you into their feed and so will likely be more receptive to your messages. For this reason it's also important not to flood their message board with non-relevant offers, or you could find yourself kicked back out into the cold. You set up a brand page through your personal Facebook account.

9

Remember to switch all your privacy settings to 'friends only' if you don't want your customers poking around in your personal life. Inviting other Facebook users to become admins will mean that they can help to update and run the brand page through their own personal account – but make sure it's someone you trust. Once you've completed the set-up, the option to choose your 'custom URL' (also known as a vanity URL, as it is easier to remember and share than the default web address issued by the system) will appear in the tips box at the top of the page; for example, you can find this book's brand page at Facebook.com/ WorkingTheCloud (come and 'like it' if you like it). You only get one chance to set your custom URL, so make sure that you spell it correctly.

TIP

Promote your Facebook brand page the old-fashioned way, by giving out flyers and putting signs up in shop windows. Entice customers to join you online by offering a discount code or special offer. Once you have them in your online community you can build on that relationship directly to create a really strong customer loyalty bond.

twitter.com

The other social network you are likely to have heard of is Twitter. Many people are confused by Twitter and don't know how to use it. Individuals sign up and treat it like some kind of popularity contest, using the 'follow you, follow me' strategy to gain as many followers as possible. But if your followers aren't listening to you there is pretty much no point in their being there – and when you see an account that has 5,000 followers but is following 5,000+ people back, you know that anything you say is just going to get lost in the noise of thousands of people all shouting at once. For a small business the way to use Twitter is as a noticeboard for the things you've got going on elsewhere on the web – like a Facebook update or blog post. If you spend time keeping up to date with the news in your area you can also provide a helpful information service for your followers, posting and tweeting links to articles you've read that they might find useful or interesting. This will earn you respect and grow your following as they in turn share your tweets with the people who are following them (for complete Twitter beginners, this is known as 'retweeting'). Taking a little time to share the odd link will also boost your online reputation, which we'll be talking about in more detail in Chapter 3. Most popular blogs and news sites include automatic sharing buttons to all the popular social sites, so you can pass on stories that you find with just a few clicks. Be careful not to post too much irrelevant information or blatant marketing messages (referred to as 'spamming'), or you could end up damaging your reputation.

 TIP

Another great use for Twitter is keeping up to date with what your competitors are doing by following their accounts if they have them – although you might be wise to do it from your personal account if you don't want to raise any eyebrows.

www.linkedin.com

The social sites we've spoken about so far will be the way you meet your customers in the cloud, but for business-to-business (B2B) networking LinkedIn is where it's at. With over 175 million users in over 200 countries – 10 million of whom are in the UK, effectively tripling the network's user base in this country in less than three years – it's the third most popular social network, but has actually been shown to be four times better at generating B2B leads than Facebook and Twitter. What's really key though is that LinkedIn profiles have been shown to have a higher search 'page ranking' than any other social profile, meaning that your profile page is likely to appear near the top of the page of links if anyone searches for your services. Once you've registered your account, nab your custom web address by editing your profile. If you have registered

 TIP

If you want your LinkedIn company page address to look the same as your other online assets, leave out the spaces when typing the name. Provided that web address is still available, your URL will come up in a similar way to this: LinkedIn.com/companies/WorkingTheCloud.

with a company email domain – like kate@WorkingTheCloud.biz – you can now go to the 'Companies' page and set up your own company LinkedIn page. You'll need to have completed more than half of your profile and made 'several' connections to prove you are genuine. You can't choose a custom URL, but your page will be named automatically based on company name and what is available – for example linkedin.com/company/working-the-cloud. Now you're set up you can invite other people whom you trust to help run the page as administrators. If you don't have a company email address you can still make your presence known professionally by starting a LinkedIn 'Group' page.

 TIP

www.linkedinlabs.com
Visit LinkedIn Labs, where you'll find lots of extra features that you can add to your experience – from services to help veterans look for work based on military credentials, to CV makers and analysis tools for spotting any genuine sales leads in the everyday chatter of hundreds of status updates.

plus.google.com

If you're already breaking out in a cold sweat at the thought of registering another social site, you could stop there; but if you have the stamina, I strongly advise that you consider a couple more. Google Plus has been far more successful than Google's previous attempts at going social, but is still pretty small fry compared with a billion people using Facebook. At the time of writing Google Plus has over 400 million registered users, 100 million of them active on a monthly basis. When you consider that this is a little over a year since opening its doors to the public, that makes Google Plus the fastest-growing social network in history. Significantly, too, current studies show that 60% of active users log in daily and 80% weekly, so the overall level of engagement seems to be among the highest. For the time being, though, it is still considered by many to be more of a niche network, tending to attract a slightly geekier user base.

TIP

gplus.to
At the time of writing, Google has just started rolling out vanity URLs to some of the more high-profile pages, such as David Beckham and Britney Spears, and even BBC Click, for which I report on web developments. Now anyone with over 1,000 followers can request their page is verified and given a custom URL. Alternatively, gplus.to provides a service for creating your own short URL – for example gplus.to/WorkingTheCloud. Just add the name for which you want to check availability, and then copy that long string of numbers from your Google Plus page URL to use as your ID.

So why should you nab your name? For starters, if you could call your business anything close to niche or slightly geeky, you will find a very receptive audience here. You will get kudos from them for existing on their favoured network, too. With 25% of users registered as students, this is a good network for connecting with that demographic. And if you use any of Google's other products, such as Gmail, Docs, Search, YouTube (we'll be talking more about these in later chapters), it's worth adding this one to the list for the product integration and convenience of a unified login. Just registering your Google Plus page will turn out to be a very smart move for marketing your business, as we'll discuss more in Chapter 2.

TIP

Group your Google Plus connections using the 'Circles' feature, thus giving you plenty of control when it comes to targeting your audience. You may not have time to personalise each message, but if you sort your audience by gender or some other defining characteristic you can address the group using the right vernacular so as to make them feel that you've made a personal effort.

Once you've registered – which must be done using a person's name, or you run the risk of your account being temporarily suspended later on – you can create a company page, which you customise with a banner, profile image and text in the same way as your Facebook brand page. Invite other people to help run the page as administrators if you trust them.

TIP

For a fantastic example of how Google Plus can be used to engage a lot of customers simultaneously, check out Cadbury UK's page at www. google.com/+CadburyUK. It currently has over 2.2 million fans, yet the posts all feel very chatty and approachable. No heavy-handed marketing tactics here, just useful advice and some rather delicious-looking images.

youtube.com

While we're on a social roll there is one last domain that you should consider: YouTube. You may not think that you'll have any videos to post, but as we explore various options for getting the word out in later chapters, you may change your view on that. Besides, if you've already registered a Google account, occupying your YouTube real estate is just a few clicks away, so it seems foolish not to grab it now – just in case. Once logged in to YouTube you'll find the option to set your vanity channel URL under 'Channel Settings/Info and Settings'. Like most vanity URL options, you can set this only once, so double-check for typos before hitting 'OK'.

ONLINE IDENTITY SNATCHERS

What to do if your online identity is already being used

So what if someone else is using your name? For completely legitimate reasons other people may be using the same trading name as you. If you think that you have a claim under trademark infringement you're probably going to need legal advice. There are good resources for researching your options and rights online. The place for UK businesses to go is www.ipo.gov.uk, and if you do a quick search you will find that most progressive governments around the world offer similar online services.

If it's just a case of another individual using the same name there is pretty much nothing you can do, apart from change your own name. You may be frustrated to see that someone else has registered a Twitter or Facebook account that you want but has not posted anything on it for years. Again, I'm afraid there is little you can do about this – and the account may not be truly inactive, as not all activity is visible; its owner could be more of a watcher than a poster. Facebook will only ever suspend an account if its owner violates the terms and conditions – and doing nothing isn't against site rules. Twitter does keep a watch out for inactive accounts, suspending them after six months, but so far it hasn't released any names to be reused. The current entry in Twitter's help section says it is "working to release all inactive usernames in bulk, but we do not have a set time frame for when this will take place". Follow @support on Twitter to be updated when inactive usernames become available.

The other possibility, although a rare one, is that someone is deliberately 'squatting' on your name. This could be for competitive reasons, or it could be something more sinister, like malicious posting or profiteering. All the networks that we've looked at so far expressly forbid impersonation and will usually act swiftly if you have a solid case, although Twitter states quite clearly in its help section that "we will not release inactive or squatted usernames except in cases of trademark infringement" – which could end up leaving an ugly hole in your online portfolio even if you do get the imposter closed down.

 TIP

If someone already has your ID and you can't change your company name, you're going to have to settle for a slight variation, like adding some numbers or an underscore. Make sure that whatever name you choose is available across ALL the networks that you want to sign up with before making a start.

Profile

Seth Casteel, Little Friends Lifestyle Pet Photography

"It's important to seize the opportunity with both hands. You have a limited window, like winning the lottery, but you only have a few days to get back to the shop and collect on your ticket before it expires."

One person who knows the value of the social web is Seth Casteel, proprietor of a small pet photography business in Los Angeles. At the end of 2011 he was struggling to get enough business to pay the bills so he did what every great entrepreneur should do; he blew his last couple of thousand bucks on some underwater camera equipment. He went on to take some brilliantly comical photographs of dogs diving into a swimming pool, chasing after toys. After he posted them on his website they went viral over one weekend, shared on Google Plus and the hugely popular links-sharing site Reddit, where they earned nearly 30,000 'likes' in a couple of days and were shared almost 22,000 times. Traffic on Seth's website sky-rocketed overnight and the increased publicity completely turned his business around, generating print sales in over 40 countries and allowing him to raise his commissioned portrait fee and fill his diary with bookings many times over; he even appeared on UK television series *Top Dog Model*, capturing the contestants' underwater style. On top of this, Seth's first book, *Underwater Dogs*, was published and distributed in over 100 countries in October 2012. It showcases more than 80 gorgeous underwater dog photographs filled with passion and personality, including 12-week-old puppies, a brilliant pug dog and even a wolf, and makes a perfect coffee table gift book, even if you're not a massive dog lover.

Seth said:

This all started when I was commissioned to take photos of a King Charles spaniel called Buster, who spent the entire photo shoot jumping into the pool chasing after a tennis ball. My work is all about capturing a dog's personality, so I thought: "This is Buster, this is his story, so I may as well photograph him in the pool and the best way to do that would be from underwater." So I bought a point-and-shoot waterproof camera and started experimenting. When I got more serious and bought the underwater camera housing for a few thousand dollars my friends said I was an idiot – I could hardly even afford to pay my bills. But I am in this business because I love it and I'm here to take chances and try to be an entrepreneur, so I took a chance. It turned out to be a lucky break for me and it's been completely overwhelming. I've always tried to embrace social media and had a Facebook page for a long time but it took me several years of regular posting and spending time and effort to get people following me before I got 6,000 'likes'. When the underwater dogs series went viral my number of followers grew to 120,000 organically in a couple of months, which is mind-blowing to me. One of the reasons I like using Facebook is I can talk directly to people in a specific area, with a specific interest. So if I am heading to Phoenix to do a photo shoot I can run a campaign targeting my client database of people aged 29 to 65 who like golden retrievers and live within a 50-mile radius of Phoenix, and then send them a picture of a golden retriever that I've taken, alerting them that I will be in Phoenix on a particular date and available for a few bookings to do commissioned portraits of their dogs. I used to print flyers and hand out business cards in dog-walking parks and at car washes, but this is much more effective! It's hard to prepare for something like this; I went from 200 unique visitors a day on my website to millions. If I did it again I would prepare for that traffic much better; my website at the time was built using Flash, so it couldn't be viewed on an iPhone or iPad and it wasn't set up to allow unlimited concurrent connections, so a lot of people couldn't get onto my site. You have to be very careful with your hosting service in cases like this; if you open up the floodgates and you have a contract where you are paying for bandwidth and you suddenly have 5 million people downloading your photographs, you might end up with a bill for $100,000 in a day – this has actually happened to people. The power of the Internet is phenomenal, and it's something that I wasn't really able to understand until this all happened. If I could go back and do it all again, apart from preparing my website technically, I would tell myself to hire more people to help; especially with publicity and establishing my brand. If this happens to you it is important to seize the opportunity with both hands. You have a limited window, like winning the lottery but you only have a few days to get back to the shop and collect on your ticket before it expires.

www.littlefriendsphoto.com
You can check out Seth's amazing photography for yourself on his website, where you'll find links to his Facebook page to see how he interacts so successfully with his followers – a lot can be learned just by observing the good work of others. You'll also find links to order your own copy of his book, *Underwater Dogs*, which would make a brilliant addition to anyone's coffee table collection.

PICTURE-PERFECT POSTING

How and why to share images online

Posting pictures can be a really good way to get people talking about you. People love sharing images, and social sites like Pinterest allow users to pin collections of things they like to a central page, linking back to the original website if people want to know more. Being linked on popular sites like this can drive your company name up a Google search enquiry, something we'll be discussing in great detail when we tackle search engine optimisation in Chapter 2. If your business is about creating something that looks good, you should definitely consider taking your camera out regularly and uploading a snap to your social networks. Around 300 million photos are uploaded to Facebook every day, and if your work catches the imagination of the online public, they could spread the word far and wide on your behalf – and Facebook is just one of many great photo-sharing networks online. You do need to be a little careful about giving away too much – always read the terms of any sharing platform in case you are giving up your intellectual property rights by posting images on the network. We'll cover copyright issues in more depth in Chapter 3.

instagram.com

Your photos don't have to be professional quality, although a really bad picture can do more harm to you than good. You can take some lovely, arty shots with your smartphone if you have the right apps installed. There are dozens of great-quality choices, depending on the look you're after, and they're mostly free to download. Instagram is without doubt the most popular photographic smartphone app currently available on Apple and Android handsets. It includes a range of retro 'instamatic' effect filters and auto-posting to Facebook, Twitter and a couple of other social platforms that you might need later on. The app has been so successful, racking up over a billion snaps in the first two years of operation, that Facebook bought the company for $1 billion in 2012. We will no doubt see even more seamless integration between Facebook and Instagram in the years ahead.

TIP

picmarkr.com
Protect your intellectual property by 'watermarking' photos that you don't want people to download and share without giving you credit. You can do this fairly easily using an image tool like Photoshop, or free alternative GIMP, which we'll look at in Chapter 5. If you'd rather have a website do it for you automatically, you can make a pretty unsophisticated watermark online at picmarkr.com.

BURYING YOUR HEAD IN THE CLOUD

Information resources for every start-up and small business

Regardless of whether you end up being active on the social web or not, it's important to have a presence in those places even if it just directs visitors to a telephone number or postal address. As I mentioned earlier, a significant portion of the general public turns to the Internet first when searching for a local business, so you're literally throwing away leads if you ignore it. Even if you don't want to engage socially online, there are plenty of valuable resources that you can make use of to gain an advantage over your competitors. There are dozens of fantastic websites full of free advice, guides and inspirational features and profiles, aimed at encouraging more people to succeed in business.

www.startups.co.uk

Startups.co.uk is a site packed with great reading for anyone setting up a business. From franchising to going green, there are step-by-step guides on every topic, including finance, sales and marketing and even what IT equipment you'll need. This website also recognises local business by running an annual awards ceremony, which you should definitely consider entering for a little extra exposure and some free publicity.

 TIP

Sponsored awards can be a great way of gaining recognition that can be turned into free publicity by sending a press release to your local newspaper or radio station. They generally love to talk about local businesses winning awards and might even ask you to come in for an interview, which is a golden opportunity for great local exposure.

www.syob.co.uk

Short for Start Your Own Business, syob.co.uk has an interesting approach, letting you specify a UK location before it makes a graphical booklet with links to all the right government departments and advisory services for your region. There's plenty of more general advice to read and follow, too, ultimately giving you a step-by-step manual for setting up your own business. It's ideal for those reluctant technophobes who are reading this book because they realise that they may find the traditional 'magazine style' layout of the booklet a little more palatable. You can even print it out if you want to be a total Luddite. The website also has a vibrant and supportive community, with plenty of additional web content to enjoy.

www.companybug.co.uk

For those thinking about setting up a limited company there are plenty of websites offering free, straightforward advice and links to the services and government departments they'll need. Company Bug is a good resource, updated regularly with articles and news and with guides covering everything from 'the benefits of running a limited company' to tax and legal requirements or dealing with contractors. If you're still not sure whether it's worth the hassle of setting up a limited company you could look at joining an 'umbrella company' – a good choice for freelancers and sole traders, as the company acts as an employer to agency contractors working under fixed-term contract assignments. There is a useful guide on Company Bug to help you identify and compare the umbrella companies that you should consider joining.

www.marketingdonut.co.uk

Marketing Donut is a great example of the kind of specialist interest network that you can find if you look around. Obviously the focus here is UK marketing, but you can find any number of other topics covered, from all over the world. The site regularly publishes articles that will help you understand how to catch your customers' eyes – or you can dip into the directory of professionals if you'd rather hire a local expert to do your marketing for you.

 TIP

Even if someone appears in a respected directory listed as an 'expert', you should still take time to check into their background and credentials. A simple Google search on their name or company can be very revealing if someone has a reputation for being unreliable.

FEEDING THE CLOUD
Places to find and share valuable business resources

The Internet exists as it does today because it is human nature to want to share things. We also generally seek out a tribe, somewhere we can fit in and be accepted for the value we bring to the group. Open source knowledge-sharing sites, where people come to post their thoughts and findings free for anyone else to use and share, are like the public libraries of the World Wide Web. Perhaps the most famous example of this is Wikipedia, though you'll have heard mixed opinions on the accuracy of its information if you spend any time online. On the whole, I find Wikipedia is a good place to start for a snapshot of a topic, but you should definitely not take everything you read there as gospel truth. Posts are often meticulously linked to source data, so you can go off and validate the information yourself if you're going to quote it. But for business there are some very effective knowledge-sharing sites that could save you hours of slaving over a depressing PowerPoint presentation or trying to devise an airtight contract. If it needs doing, making, or even thinking about, you can bet there are dozens of people who have already done, made or thought about it and have shared the outcome online. We're going to be talking more about collaborating in these kinds of communities in Chapter 9, but for now I want to show you a couple of places where you might find useful resources for your own business.

www.slideshare.net

If you've ever found yourself nodding off during a conference talk or business presentation, you'll know that creating a good slide show is an art form in its own right. If the thought of wrestling with a program like PowerPoint or Keynote to come up with something original makes you glaze over inside a little, take some time to see what's available on SlideShare. With over 60 million visitors and 130 million page views a month, it's the go-to network for sharing professional presentations — which is probably why LinkedIn bought the company for over $100 million in 2012. Users can upload presentations privately if they have a premium account, but a lot of the content is put on the site publicly for others to use free of charge. It's like YouTube for presentations, and includes a handy 'embed code' feature that you can use if you want to re-post a slide show on your own website or blog.

> **TIP**
>
> *An 'embed code' is a snippet of software that you can copy from the website where you're hosting content and paste into another web page – such as your blog. This makes the content appear inside your website rather than visitors having to leave your domain and go to watch it on the host's website.*

www.scribd.com

Scribd is newer to the market, but catching up fast. It offers a very similar service, and if you're searching for something specific you should probably check both sites for the perfect fit. If you're going to be uploading any content yourself for use in promotional campaigns, you should probably go for Scribd, as the in-depth analytics (something we'll speak about more in Chapter 3) are free, whereas you'll need a premium account in order to gain any insight on SlideShare.

www.docstoc.com

A much smaller concern, Docstoc is still worth looking at, as it focuses on building a database of professional, financial and legal documents for the business community, presented in a way that is optimised for small business needs. There are sample documents for pretty much every occasion, whether you're putting together a consulting agreement or want to create a professional employee contract. There are even customisable templates for legal documents that have been created by professionals, though you'll need to pay for a premium account to download them.

snapguide.com

Snapguide is a fun new addition that lets people make quick and easy step-by-step photographic guides using a free iPhone app, or by uploading photographs through a web browser. Many of the guides are quite trivial and fun, but there is some pretty useful content in there too. Making your own guides, to embed on your website or link to through social platforms, can be another very effective way of engaging with your customers. I'm sure that heating engineers must get called out all the time to relight the pilot flame (I use this example as I've done it myself, but you can extrapolate the analogy to fit many trades). It's hardly worth their time travelling to the customer without charging an unsavoury call-out fee, potentially souring the relationship. That same heating engineer could throw together a guide on how to reignite the pilot light and post it on Facebook, directing any floundering customers there. I think I know which heating engineer the customers are going to call when their boiler finally does need replacing!

 TIP

Contributing useful content to knowledge-sharing sites is a great way to build online reputation and draw more members to your social networks. Once potential customers are following you, any marketing messages that you publish in those feeds will appear in their daily notices.

A CLOUD WITH A VIEW

What does the Internet know about you?

As we'll explore in the chapters to come, the Internet can tell you a lot about your customers, which could provide valuable insight into how to engage with them more effectively. But it can also tell you quite a lot about yourself. Google, the undisputed king of web-page indexing, can probably tell you the most, and the company has spent a lot of time and money creating slick analytics tools to help you (and it) understand the web better.

www.google.com/dashboard

Access your Google Dashboard by logging in at Google.com/dashboard, which then connects all the data from your various Google accounts, including Search, Docs, YouTube, Google Plus and others. The Dashboard displays all your recent Google account activity on one page, which can save a lot of time logging in and out of multiple sites when you want to review things. You can also sign up for regular account activity reports, which you find through the Dashboard by clicking 'Accounts' and then choosing 'Products' from the sidebar. The service will generate a report every few days, with a monthly round-up containing more insight to help you streamline your activity.

TIP

www.google.com/ads/preferences
Google makes certain assumptions based on your online activity, which it uses to serve up more targeted advertisements. To know who Google thinks you are, check out Google.com/ads/preferences. In my own case, Google thinks I am a male aged 24–34. If you want to see ads that might be more relevant to you, you can change your demographics and add or remove areas of interest on this page.

ONCE MORE INTO THE CLOUD, MY FRIEND

You should now have all the information you need to kick-start your business and get the essential online properties registered and ready to work with. With these core essentials sorted, you are well on the way to getting the Internet working for your business – not bad for a few hours of filling out registration forms and setting up your profiles. Having established a presence on the World Wide Web, in the chapters to come we're going to be tackling some aspects in more detail, such as marketing and promotion, business management and finance tools, and dozens of fantastic ways to save time and money without damaging the quality of your work. Small businesses are a key part of the UK economy, accounting for around half of all business turnover and paying around a third of all taxes. Competition from the cloud will only get tougher as lean, efficient micro-businesses operating out of 'virtual offices' and using cloud technology to the best advantage continue snatching market share. If you want to experience growth in the years ahead, harnessing the power of the Internet is your best bet – and *Working the Cloud* contains all the tools and advice that you need to win.

Chapter 2
A social explosion

Social media and self-promotion tools and techniques

In this chapter we're going to look at ways in which you can find and engage with your potential customers, local and national – even global, if that's the way you want your business to grow – offering them direct incentives to drive more traffic to your online properties to check out your wares. We'll also talk about 'social recommendation' and 'influence', and how you can improve yours by implementing some very simple and genuine techniques to help raise your company's name towards the top of local search results. This business practice is called 'search engine optimisation' or SEO, and you'll come across plenty of companies in your area offering their professional services to achieve results. Whole bibles have been written on the subject, and I could never hope to compete with them in just a few pages. Instead, consider the entries in this chapter as a 'belt-and-braces' checklist of all the simple yet highly effective techniques that you can implement for yourself to get the online visibility ball rolling. We'll be covering:

- why you can't ignore the social web
- dealing with negative feedback or malicious comments on your social sites
- how to plan the perfect social media marketing campaign
- how to avoid conflict and arguments online
- connecting with specialist networks that might have a keen interest in your business

- online communities designed to make real-world connections
- more detailed tips and resources for using Facebook and Twitter
- an interview with Theo Paphitis, serial entrepreneur and former *Dragons' Den* investor
- recommendation platforms and getting noticed online.

WORKING THE CROWD

Finding and engaging with your customers online

Staking your claim on the social web means that people can now find you, even if you're not really talking to them. You've joined more than half of all small businesses, and that figure is growing rapidly as more people catch on to how easy it is to get publicity if you use the right tactics. At this stage I should probably apologise to anyone who is still in denial about the importance of using social media, because these days it's very much a case of 'if you can't join them, they will beat you'. If the most active global virtual communities were countries, here's what the world map might look like (approximately) according to population.

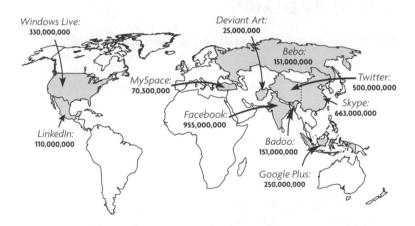

So everybody's at it, and you should be too. But that doesn't mean that you have to spend hours each day coming up with pithy status updates and chatting to any Tom, Dick or Harry who might buy something from you. It also doesn't have to involve spending a single penny on advertising, as we'll discover later in this chapter.

So who is this 'crowd' that everyone keeps talking about? It's a term that you're going to hear a lot if you embrace the social web. As in life, a crowd is a large group of people with some shared characteristic or purpose. On the Internet that normally means signing up to something like a 'crowd-funding' project, where ordinary people can contribute in some way towards the financial needs of a start-up business (which we'll talk about in some detail in Chapter 10). Other crowds form to collect and distribute vast amounts of information– free and often fast. It's called 'crowd sourcing', and the most high-profile cases normally come to light during disaster relief efforts, such as when road maps of rural Haiti were urgently needed by international rescue teams following the devastating earthquake in 2010. Wikipedia is a crowd-sourced online encyclopaedia.

Projects like this have attracted crowds in their thousands – in the case of Wikipedia, tens of millions have been involved in writing it – but you don't need to be thinking anything close to that scale to give your small business a real boost.

SOCIAL BY DESIGN

How to plan a successful social media campaign

GOAL > STRATEGY > TACTICS

The very first thing that you need is a goal, and then you can come up with a strategy to reach it. It doesn't have to be a very grand, long-term goal. In fact, if you're just starting out on the social web I would advise that you set your sights quite low to begin with, as the bigger picture will happen on its own if you get the small stuff right. It might seem a bit obvious, but before you go spamming the hell out of your networks and confusing them, work out what it is that you want to achieve. If you're a retailer that might mean getting 15% more customers to visit your shop on a Wednesday; if you're in a trade it could be quoting for 10 new jobs a week. Whatever outcome suits your business, decide on your first short-term goal now. Sorted?

Good.

With a goal in mind you should be able to picture your target demographic; now you just need a strategy to hook them. Maybe that will be offering a discount voucher for days when your business is quiet. Perhaps you'd rather run a competition, or build a buzz around a launch event. Running meaningful promotions and give-aways used to be the exclusive domain of much larger companies, as you need a decent-sized audience to sell to. But the rise of social media over the last half decade has opened up the playing field. Using the right tactics – the final piece of your social media game plan – you can gather an audience through your networks and then slam them all right between the eyes at the same moment with your offer. If it's well received your followers will share it and recommend it to their own networks, and you will see your exposure blossom organically inside whichever groups you have targeted.

So, in the example of a retail outlet that wants to see more customers through the door on a quiet day, the following broad campaign design would work well:

GOAL: Increase footfall by 15% on Wednesdays.

STRATEGY: Advertise a promotion for Wednesdays to 500 potential new customers.

TACTICS: Connect and engage with existing customers online; post content and offers to further engage customers and get them spreading the word about you to their own networks; use flyers and postcards to entice new customers to join you online.

I'm paraphrasing massively there, and the example is only one amongst countless possible campaign objectives. Don't worry: throughout this book we'll be talking about individual strategies and tactics as we explore the tools to help you execute them. For now, though, having that simple structure in mind and a very definite goal in your sights will make time spent online far more rewarding.

TIP

If one of your direct competitors is doing well, scour through their social accounts to see what tactics they are employing. It might feel a bit dirty, but competitor research is a perfectly valid business strategy, and made so much easier by the Internet. If they don't have any social accounts, this is your chance to get several leaps ahead of them.

NOT EVERY CLOUD HAS A SILVER LINING

Dealing with negative feedback and malicious comments

You're going to hear me talk a lot about the positive aspects of being online, but it's worth remembering that this direct link to your customers works in both directions — a fact that will probably only truly hit home when you get your first serious complaint. If people are saying things on your social pages that you don't like, as the administrator you have the ability (and right) to hide or even delete their comments. Some people just post stupid stuff to get attention. It's best just to ignore these people, and they will go away eventually. The moment you engage with them they get their reward, so will likely do it again. On all of the main social platforms you can ban certain users if their objectionable behaviour persists. In extreme cases, or if you believe that you are being subjected to defamation or abuse, you should report the user to the website's customer services team and let it handle things for you.

If a complaint is genuine you have a couple of choices. The brave choice is to turn that negative into a positive, negotiating with the customer for a favourable outcome in public, where they posted the criticism. Remember, that's a disgruntled customer from whom you probably would never have heard again were it not for the social web. If you can turn them around to be a satisfied customer, in full view of all your other customers, it will earn you a lot of respect.

If you think that the customer might be unreasonable, or the conversation get too heated, you are much better off locking or hiding the post and taking the discussion to a private forum, by email or direct messages within the platform where they made the complaint. Never, ever get involved in a public argument, no matter how in the right you are. It never, *ever* works out for businesses. The last thing you need is a comment that you made in the public domain to go viral for all the wrong reasons, as that will be the first thing that people see when they search for you, for months, possibly even years, to come. Google, the most-used search engine by a long shot, uses a complicated algorithm to decide which links are most relevant and useful when you conduct a search. It's called 'Page Rank', and one of the things that will turbo-boost a web page up the rankings is when influential websites link to it (later in this chapter we'll look at how to use this to your advantage). Imagine if one of the satirical blogs with hundreds of thousands of readers linked to a hasty tweet that you sent one night when a customer had annoyed you. It might have been funny, or cutting, or even fair. But do you really want that to be the first thing that people see when they Google your company?

I didn't think so.

PLAYING NICELY

Online etiquette to keep you out of trouble

The evolution of human nature online is a subject much debated and often lamented. I kind of die a little inside when people start talking about 'netiquette', a pretentious contraction that basically means online etiquette. The rules should be exactly as in real life; in fact, they are. It's just that some idiots use the security blanket of anonymity to make their obtuse opinions known in public. In some ways I'm thankful that at least people like this are out in the open online. I'm sure that they mutter away to trusted friends behind closed doors in the physical world, but you'd never know it if you passed them in the street. There is nothing you can do about these people other than not become one of them, and block them from your sight or report them wherever applicable. Occasionally it won't be possible to block them, and that's where your big old internal 'ignore button' comes into play – unless you want to get known for starting an Internet 'flame war', that is.

So, as in life, treat the people you meet online like the humans they are (and ignore the ones who clearly aren't). Remember that everything you post in the public domain remains there forever. Even if you've deleted a tweet or post, someone may have already shared it, so you are never truly guaranteed that it's gone. If you decide to join any discussion forums it's a good idea to observe the activity for a few days first; get to know what tone and banter levels are the norm, and it could save you a red-faced moment if you over-react. One of the biggest sins that you can commit on a message board is to ask a common question that has been answered thoroughly elsewhere, usually several times. Regular members of these communities invest a great deal of personal time in making them the valuable resources they are, and rocking up asking a question that's covered in the FAQs just tells them that you've made zero effort. But it's worth persevering with this kind of seemingly elitist community if the subject is relevant to your business. By posting helpful comments you can gain new followers (and add a couple more points to your SEO, which we'll be discussing soon); and if it's information you're after, they provide a direct link to highly specialised experts who will consult with you one to one over a prolonged period of time, for nothing more than the kudos of being able to help.

The other thing that drives me a little crazy online is the overuse of acronyms – especially when it's me that's using them, a nasty habit I have picked up in trying to make more fit into a 140-character tweet. If you don't have to abbreviate for space reasons, don't. Ever. Because it just looks lazy. This might sound like my own personal rant, and maybe it is a little, but the Internet is full of pedants who will be very quick to jump on badly composed posts. A little care and attention to detail will go a long way towards winning them over. However, there are some acronyms that you will see all the time, so you may as well know what people are talking about.

POPULAR INTERNET ACRONYMS AND WHAT THEY REALLY MEAN
- LOL – laughs out loud (they think you're funny)
- LMFAO – laughing my **** ass off (they think you're hilarious)
- OMG – Oh my God (you shocked them)
- TMI – too much information (you really shocked them)
- WTF – what the ****? (they are shocked and have a potty mouth)

- BTW – by the way (they forgot to tell you something earlier)
- AFAIK – as far as I know (they are smugly confident they are correct)
- IMHO – in my humble opinion (they don't really care what you think)
- BRB – be right back (they've gone to do something more interesting)
- AFK – away from keyboard (they are really bored with you and have left the room)
- GR8 – pronounced 'great' (they are living in the 1990s)
- OIC – pronounced 'Oh, I see' (you just won the argument)
- IRL – in real life (they are deluded – people who use this many acronyms have no real life)

TIP

'Flaming' and 'trolling' are terms used to describe posting a deliberately antagonistic comment in someone's conversation thread. People who do this are often called 'trolls'. Some people seem to see this practice as a kind of sport, especially in large, active community groups where there is a sizeable audience to impress (or wind up).

SPECIAL INTEREST GROUPS

High-value networking opportunities with smaller online groups

In Chapter 1 we spoke about specialist social networks where any small business can go for advice and support from experts and their peers. In this chapter we're going to be looking at some different specialist networks, those that connect you with potential customers or people you might want to do business with. They are many and varied – too much for this humble book to cover completely – so I have cherry-picked a few great examples to whet your appetite for what's out there and will suggest some places and techniques that you can use to track down your own specific specialist groups. After connecting with potential customers in various scattered places you can start driving traffic towards your central hub of social operations, so that you have only one main site to check daily. Entice them to join you with offers, or the promise of more regular, interesting links and articles.

ESTABLISHED GROUPS AND NETWORKS

Finding people with a specialist interest in your business

There are thousands of sites hosting special interest groups that have been set up by members of the public and businesses alike. Arguably the best way to find something specific is by conducting a web search for it. For example, you could search for the term 'vegan community group in London' and retrieve links to a very targeted selection of networks, with the most popular usually appearing at the top. If you just want to browse by discussion topic, key word or location, there are probably three main sites you should look at:

groups.google.com

uk.groups.yahoo.com

answers.microsoft.com/communities

All of these services are free to use, similar to operate, and have their own special features and benefits. It's worth noting that pretty much all social networks survive on paid advertising, and having a niche community to serve up highly targeted ad banners to is prime Internet real estate. It's also worth considering that if you're touting for new business in someone else's group you need to tread very carefully. It might have been set up by a competitor, in which case spamming their message board with marketing is going to get you banned pretty quickly. Even if it's just run by a hobbyist or enthusiast, ease into the group gently and find ways to contribute and be helpful before talking up your business. I would advise strongly against posting any direct marketing messages on a hobby board until you know the community very well and know that what you're offering will be of interest to them. Woo them with pithy remarks and links to helpful resources (like this book, even!) in the hope that they will join you on your own social networks where you can tell them about your business more freely. A socially active group in a targeted interest area is the perfect ready-made audience – you just have to find a way of getting them into your theatre.

TIP

It's easy to start a Facebook, Google Plus or LinkedIn group to complement your business – for example, if you were selling wool you could start a group called 'Love2Knit'. Attract members by sharing articles and free patterns. It needn't cost you anything or take much time if you like to surf for this kind of content anyway. You now have a ready group of consumers being regularly reminded about your brand, and you can promote the odd offer to them too.

QUESTION AND ANSWER (Q&A) COMMUNITIES

How answering a few simple questions can boost your reputation

There is also no shortage of Q&A communities thriving online. If you want to know the answer to any question you can think of, it is probably already out there, somewhere. You can ask questions yourself, but it's a good idea to run a quick search first, as you can often find that the answer already exists. For example, you could search for 'How do I run a social media campaign?', which will lead you to far more resources on the subject than I could ever cover here. You can also search for a question that you think your customers might ask – for example, a photographic supplies company could search for 'How do I take better photos?' It might turn up some current conversations and you could contribute to, hopefully impressing the community enough for people to come and join you on your social networks. By including a link to your website in your signature you will also help to push your site up through the search rankings, which I'll explain in detail when we speak about SEO. These are the most common places you will find questions being answered online:

- answers.yahoo.com
- wiki.answers.com
- ask.com
- www.quora.com

The last one is a relative newcomer, which experienced rapid growth when it caught the attention of some powerful social media influencers such as Stephen Fry and Wikipedia founder Jimmy Wales. If you're going to be contributing answers, keep things professional when you sign up by linking to it with your Twitter account rather than Facebook, as the Facebook authorisation forces you to switch back to your personal profile to make the connection.

CONNECTING WITH YOUR PEERS

Networks to meet your professional peers, on and offline

dribbble.com

Dribbble is a nice example of a more organised specialist group, with a specific purpose in mind. It allows designers to showcase their work, bouncing off each other as well as connecting with people who are interested in hiring them. A lot of the technical professions have communities like this (and a growing number of non-technical professions do too), so if you're a freelancer looking for new clients these are a great place to set up shop.

www.getlunched.com

An interesting new trend beginning to emerge is networks that connect virtual contacts in the real world. Get Lunched uses your LinkedIn contacts and lets you browse through the registered users on a map to see if anyone local has the skills you need. If you see someone with whom you want to connect you can offer to buy them lunch – you have the option of suggesting that they pay, or that the bill is split 50/50, if you think that's more appropriate – and the site will even help you to find a discounted restaurant or suitable venue close by, though you're not obliged to choose the suggestions. Now, hopefully, that accountant whom you vaguely know through LinkedIn can be persuaded to give you a bit of tax advice for the cost of a £30 lunch. You might even make a new friend and ally too.

girlgeekdinners.com, directorsof.com

Talking of lunch, there is also a growing army of dinner clubs putting on regular small dinner parties and cocktail soirées to allow local business people to network. Above are just two that I am personally aware of, as I take part occasionally. You can search for your own interest group just as easily. Some of these clubs are very popular and can attract generous product sponsors – Girl Geek Dinners parties usually have copious amounts of cupcakes littered around. You may have to listen to a few talks while you're sipping your free Pinot, but these can be very enlightening, or, if not, you can always gossip – err, network – with your neighbour. Other dinner clubs may have a monthly membership or require you to pay your share of the bill on the night (perhaps with a percentage added for administration). These are a fantastic way of building a strong business network while having fun, so could be well worth the money if you like socialising.

TIP

If you have a product to promote, contacting a small dinner group to offer samples for the goodie bag is a great way to get people talking about you online. These organisations are often very proactive in promoting their sponsors to their whole network, so you will reach a much larger audience than just those who attended.

www.meetup.com

If you don't find a group that suits you, consider starting one yourself. Meetup helps 1 million plus members to arrange 340,000 monthly meet-ups – the small monthly cost to become an 'arranger' can be shared out amongst your members. When you search for an event it will display all the registered meet-ups within 10 miles of your location; you can change the location by clicking on the link if you want to search the nearest busy town. From property developers to life coaches (and everything in between), there are groups formed here that meet up regularly to make connections.

www.yammer.com

Sometimes a public group isn't the best solution – say, if you want to keep in touch with staff or the contacts in a supply chain. Yammer has only around 5 million users, but the very specific controls that you can apply make it perfect for small, super-private groups to network.

Microsoft was so impressed that it bought the platform for more than $1 billion in 2012, so we're likely to see more integration with Microsoft's other software in the future.

WORKING YOUR BRAND PAGE

Making the most of your professional Facebook presence

Hopefully you're now talking to potential customers online, so it's time to go back to the old faithful platforms I had you register for earlier, those monoliths of the social web that by luck or design (and often a large dose of both) have become the standard relationship stock exchanges of the World Wide Web. As I write this book, Facebook has 955 million active users, although the company recently had to admit that around 8.7% might not be real. That's still over 850 million highly engaged users, though — and probably well over a billion by the time you read these numbers. There are still questions around the efficacy of Facebook's paid advertising, but as a way to collect your customers and serve them up content that might be interesting to them, it's hard to beat.

 TIP

Facebook page administrators can schedule a post to happen at a specific day and time. Use this feature to make sure that your content hits everyone's Facebook feeds when they are most likely to be watching them, maximising exposure. The busiest times are generally around 11am, 3pm and 8pm.

Here's how to use your Facebook brand page more effectively.

In terms of demographic, the largest is 21- to 24-year-olds, closely followed by 18- to 20-year-olds and 34- to 44-year-olds. So, a good spread, and the gender skew is negligible. It is important to get people to 'like' your page, as it tells Facebook that they are interested in what you have to say, so your posts will appear in their main feed. With some users having hundreds of friends, though, Facebook applies an algorithm to help filter out some of the noise in each person's feed. If your new friend doesn't interact with you occasionally by 'liking', sharing or making a comment on your posts, you will eventually drop off their reading list. To avoid this, be consistent with your posts and always encourage feedback or interaction.

TIP

Research has shown that 60% of people are willing to post about products or services on Facebook if they get a deal or discount. If you post an offer, making it open to anyone who shares your post in their own timeline – it could have an explosive effect on your reach.

Once you start to build some traffic you can use the 'Insights' tool to find out how many people your message is reaching and what they liked best. This data can be used to fine-tune your posting tactics to a lean, mean, social engagement machine – in other words, highly effective but with as little effort involved as possible.

TIP

Facebook users are most likely to share the following on their timelines: personal achievements, travel plans, buying tickets for a night out and donating to charity. Have this in mind when coming up with ideas for content that is most likely to be shared a lot.

PROMOTED POSTS

Should you pay to get your message out on Facebook?

As I mentioned earlier, there has been some media speculation about the value of Facebook's traditional paid advertisements. But the company also recently launched a 'Promoted Post' feature, which is a way to pay a small amount of cash (around $10 at the time of writing) to guarantee that your post will appear in the feeds of all the people who have 'liked' you. You will need to have gained 400 'likes' in order to access this feature, but once you have, promoting a post is so cheap that it doesn't take much thinking about. In many ways it seems foolish not to use this option if you're pushing out a big one-off promotion. Critics argue that it's not really fair on those companies that have earned their reputation the hard way, one click at a time. Where you stand on it morally is up to you, but it remains a very cheap way to reach a focused audience.

 TIP

If your page has more than 400 'likes' you can include offers in your timeline, a feature that spotlights your post in your followers' feeds and automatically shares it with the friends of anyone who decides to take you up on it. This creates a nice cascade of publicity within a targeted audience, with typically higher levels of trust involved because their friend has already endorsed the deal. The first time you run an offer it's free, after which there is a sliding scale of micropayments, depending on how big an audience you want to reach.

www.pagemodo.com

It's worth spending a bit of time getting your brand page right, as you never get a second chance to make a first impression. Choose images that are eye-catching and relevant – perhaps a logo and an arty photo of your products for the banner? Pagemodo lets you customise your page further, adding a tab with extra information on it from a range of templates: free and premium. The free account lets you manage one brand page, adding one extra tab, and with various paid sign-ups you can do more. Use that tab to share information about a particular event or product line – perhaps even directions and a map.

POWER TWEETING

Top tips and resources for making Twitter work for your business

More than one-quarter of all young adults (18- to 29-year-olds) on the Internet use Twitter, so if that's your target demographic it's an excellent place to connect with them. The 31- to 49-year-old age group is also well represented, making up over 40% of the user base. As I mentioned in Chapter 1, a lot of people have trouble figuring out how to use Twitter properly. For some it's becoming a replacement for an RSS feed, which is a piece of software that collects the day's stories from places of interest for you to read at your convenience. Others use Twitter as a tool for marketing or to spread information and articles. Some even use it to connect with friends and family, though the public nature of the platform, together with the 140-character limit for a message, makes it far from ideal for building relationships. For most, it's best for short updates that get straight to the point, with further reading usually a click away. In business it's extremely useful for monitoring conversations about your brand. If you want to use it to speak to your customers and potential customers there are a few things you need to understand; and, of course, there are some great free tools to help you manage your account more effectively. All Twitter interactions can be completed through the browser, but many people choose to use a third-party client – such as HootSuite or TweetDeck – which provides an often more customisable experience.

TWEET TO WHO?

The basic mechanics of Twitter

COMPOSE: When you compose a new tweet or share a link it will appear in the timeline of everyone who follows you. It will also be included in the search results of people looking for public tweets containing the words you have written.

REPLY: If you are replying to someone directly and place their @name at the front of a tweet, it will appear in that person's 'MENTIONS' feed, however the tweet is still publicly viewable on your Twitter homepage (for example twitter.com/WorkingTheCloud) @replies will not appear in your followers' timelines unless they are also following the recipient. If you want to reply to someone but also have it appear in everyone's feed, you just need to place one character (say a full stop) before the @ symbol.

DIRECT MESSAGE: You can send private messages using Twitter's 'Direct Message' feature. Direct messages can be sent only to people who are following you, though you do not have to be following a person to send them a direct message.

RETWEET: If someone sends you a tweet that you want to share with your followers, use the 'retweet' feature. This can be a nice way to reward your followers for engaging with you on the platform – and it is generally considered very bad form to tweet a link without giving credit to the person who shared it with you.

FAVOURITE: Marking tweets 'favourite' collects them into a separate folder where you can access them later on without having to hunt through your entire feed.

LISTS: By grouping accounts that you follow together into categories that interest you, such as 'world news', 'football' and 'recipes', you can easily dip into filtered content depending on your objective.

#HASHTAG CLOUD

What is a 'hashtag' and how can you use it?

The use of hashtags (#) is a defining characteristic of Twitter, but it was actually a practice first made popular on Internet Relay Chat (IRC) as a way of making topics and groups easier to find in a search. By putting a # in front of a word in your post it will turn up in the search results of anyone looking for that hashtag. This practice is widely used for events, sport, hobbies, celebrities and all manner of current events. There is also a growing number of Twitter tools and add-ons that use hashtags to track, pick up and organise content.

TIP

If you hang around Twitter on a Friday you'll see the #FF hashtag being used a lot. 'Follow Friday' has been a tradition since the beginning of 2009. It involves adding #FF to a post and then naming people you would like to recommend to your followers. Give value to your followers by making the people you recommend with a #FF really count– and be sure to thank anyone who #FFs you.

Reading Borough Libraries
0118 901 5950

Self Service Receipt for Borrowing

Name: 24126001225858

Title: Working the cloud : making the Internet work for you & your business

Item: 34126010900861

Due Back: 12/03/2022

Title: Sams teach yourself Unreal engine 4 game development in 24 hours

Item: 34126011195198

Due Back: Item is overdue -- Borrower has 1 item(s) overdue -- Renewals '4' exceeds policy

Total Borrowing: 1
19/02/2022 14:48:41

Thank you for using the library.

For renewals visit
www.reading.gov.uk/libraries

TWITTER TOOLS

Third-party tools and add-ons to make Twitter more powerful

followerwonk.com

There is little point in having thousands of followers if they are all cow farmers from Tennessee (unless you happen to own a cheese factory in the area, that is). Followerwonk's free services will help you to sniff out people who might be interested in your business and whom you have a chance of turning into customers. Advanced search options let you drill down into area and key words from profile biographies, which makes looking for 'cake lovers' in Brighton a lot easier. You can see stats about their reach and influence and follow them from within the app. There's also a handy comparison tool, so you can see how your Twitter account stacks up against a competitor's, cross-referencing your followers to indicate to you exactly whom you should target for new business. There are premium upgrades if you want fuller, more focused data.

wefollow.com

Followers are also pretty useless if none of them are sharing your posts or clicking your links. There are some power users out there with a lot of influence, and those are the ones whom you should be trying to get on board, sharing your messages. @StephenFry is a classic example of a power user in the tech sector. One mention or retweet from him will get a lot of attention from the crowd and instantly boost your follower count, though you should probably set your sights a little lower at first to avoid disappointment. WeFollow provides a good way of finding the tweeters with the most influence in your topic or location. Adding yourself to the database will also mean that you turn up in your categories and location when someone searches for them.

monitter.com

Monitter allows you to keep an eye on several different key words and phrases that people are tweeting about in a particular location. A lot of people will tweet asking for advice when they have a domestic emergency and don't know what to do. If you are a plumber, for example, you could turn this to your advantage by monitoring 'leaking', 'burst pipe' and 'need a plumber'. Once a column is set up you can click the 'gear' icon to open settings and set the location to within 10km of a postcode. Now, when someone tweets about a burst pipe in the loft leaking through the ceiling, our fearless plumber is ready to leap into action, saying that he can be there to fix it in 10 minutes.

commun.it

Once you've built a decent-sized following you can use a relationship management tool such as Commun.it to keep it nice and healthy. As well as useful stats about how you're tweeting and how your followers are reacting, here you can see exactly who is most engaged with you and how great their influence is. Highly engaged followers with a decent amount of influence make ideal people to send review and sample products to, as they are most likely to spread the word about your company online. The free account is limited in numbers and reporting, but should be enough to begin with and you have the option of upgrading to the paid version if you find it useful.

 TIP

Your top supporters need to feel that the relationship is a two-way street, so reward them often with retweets and @ mentions so that they feel appreciated. They may even pick up some followers from your following, which will only go towards strengthening the bond between you.

www.tweriod.com

There are many more tools that I could talk about here – just search for 'Twitter tools for business' if you want to explore on your own. But one last quick mention has to go to Tweriod. After authorising the app it will prepare a report for you about when your Twitter followers are most active, allowing you to tweet, or schedule tweets to happen, at those optimum times. The free reports are quite limited, but enough to give you a rough idea about weekend and weekday traffic. We'll be looking at tools for auto-tweeting at scheduled times when we talk about your virtual assistant in Chapter 7.

Profile

Theo Paphitis, Star of Dragons' Den

"Hundreds of years ago a gentleman's wealth was judged by the size of his library, because if you had knowledge you had power – it was as simple as that. Now with technology everyone's got knowledge just by using their mobile phone."

As one of Britain's most popular entrepreneurs, Theo Paphitis hardly needs an introduction. Billed on the BBC's *Dragons' Den* as a 'retail magnate', he first cut his teeth in a retail environment running the school tuck shop at the age of 15 – a role that, by his own account, was mostly designed to keep him out of trouble. He went on to become known as a bit of a 'turnaround king', reviving the fortunes of brands like La Senza (which he sold in 2006), Ryman Stationery, Red Letter Days and even Millwall football club. Seemingly having developed an eye for great lingerie, Theo's most recent high-profile retail initiative is the launch of the Boux Avenue chain of lingerie shops with an interactive website at bouxavenue.com. Most people will recognise him from the TV, but what you might not know is that Theo donates the fees from his TV appearances, speeches and sales of his biography (*Enter the Dragon*, published by Orion Books) to causes close to his heart, especially children's charities. He is also a big supporter of small businesses and entrepreneurship, providing many fantastic online resources and social media initiatives designed to give up-and-coming young businesses a leg-up. One such initiative is 'Small Business Sunday', where six lucky businesses get to ride on the back of Theo's fame by having a tweet about their company shared with his 270,000-strong Twitter following – an opportunity that can create a real buzz of free publicity, as Theo explained when we spoke.

Theo said:

The hardest thing in the world when you're running your own business is loneliness and when I got into Twitter a few years ago I found a lot of small businesses were tweeting me, so I decided to run a club to provide support and someone to speak to when they are feeling down or lonely (as we all do sometimes). I called it 'Small Business Sunday' because I remember when my own business was just starting out and every Sunday night, after putting the kids to bed, I would sit down and plan the week ahead. It was a key time because when I arrived for work on Monday morning I could hit the ground running. As well as building a supportive community and resources on the website I started running a weekly Twitter campaign between 5pm and 7.30pm on a Sunday with the hashtag #SBS. People can tweet me about their business and I pick six that I retweet to all my followers. They also get a place on our website and a photograph with me – which, because I am 'the man off the telly', can be used to get free PR and marketing. It's not an endorsement of their company but I've been very fortunate, so I don't care how they want to use the opportunity to help their own businesses. Practically without exception, all of my winners have appeared in the local newspapers and quite a few of them have appeared on local radio; some have even managed to get themselves on national radio – just by leveraging the fact that they sent a tweet and it got retweeted to hundreds of thousands of other people. That's great marketing.

Hundreds of years ago a gentleman's wealth was judged by the size of his library, because if you had knowledge you had power – it was as simple as that. Now with technology everyone's got knowledge just by using their mobile phone; you can access every bit of information that exists on the web; you can have a worldwide shop from your bedroom; you can do things that weren't even dreamt of when I started off in business. It's why technology is the most wonderful thing for small businesses. You don't need to have a unique idea – very few people have that eureka moment, so throw away the rubber duck and get out of the bath before you go all wrinkly. Instead, look around you for inspiration; look at what other people are doing and see if you can do it better; identify markets that are not cluttered and where there is an opportunity for you to make a living. One of the best businesses I invested in from *Dragons' Den* was Magic Whiteboard. It's not an invention, it's not an original product; they ship it in and they sell it. It's not an 'idea' but they've done incredibly well from it. A lot of people complicate business, but one of the things I love about *Dragons' Den* is how it simplifies business and shows it the way it is – and rightly so, because at the end of the day basic business principles are very simple. The thing I preach constantly is don't think 'I'm an entrepreneur, I take risks'. Entrepreneurs don't take risks. They take calculated risks. So do your homework and make sure you stack the cards in your favour. Fifty per cent of businesses fail in the first couple of years – why would you want to be one of those statistics? If you do your homework and keep persevering with determination, desire, drive and hard work, you can really shorten those odds and have every chance of succeeding, so don't lose faith.

(Photo courtesy of James Stroud)

www.smarta.com

One of the business websites that Theo invested in is Smarta, a support and advice network for small business owners and entrepreneurs. The business-builder platform will cost you £20 a month if you want a neat, unified solution for running your business, but there is also plenty of great free content and articles if you're just browsing. The website also runs the annual Smarta 100 awards, another opportunity to turn recognition of your business innovation into great PR through interviews with local news stations, so never shy away from entering yourself for an event like this.

www.theopaphitissbs.com

As we've already discovered, Theo Paphitis's Small Business Sunday houses a fantastic community for sharing your trials and successes with like-minded people – and you might get the chance to star in the weekly #SBS tweet-up. This could potentially generate a lot of free PR, so be ready to capitalise on the opportunity if it lands in your lap. All the small businesses joining the site put up profile pages with their own tips and discoveries learnt while running a small business, so even if you're too shy to join in you could learn a lot from just browsing other people's pages – and, of course, reading the many articles and guides provided free to the website's members.

 Profile

Henry Iddon, Freelance Photographer

Henry is a location photographer of action sports, architecture, modern lifestyles and reportage, and proud #SBS winner and community member.

Henry said:

Although I have been active in social media for some time it is often difficult to distil the connections made into something organised. What #SBS has done is formalise my online conversations with other #SBS winners, creating a tangible network for conversation and advice. While I cannot yet attribute any specific increase in revenue to #SBS, what I do know is that it has increased my confidence and broadened the type of business I am speaking with, which in due course should bring increased revenue. I've always been of the view that new business occurs through personal contact, and while social media is great for dialogue with everyone in cyberspace it doesn't necessarily result in traditional face-to-face meetings with potential clients. In the North West we now have a #SBS group on LinkedIn and have made plans for regular networking meetings where we can talk business in person, which I'm sure will bond us as an #SBS family.

THE RECOMMENDATION ENGINE

Making online recommendations networks work for you

If you've ever bought anything from Amazon you may have noticed the 'social recommendation engine' at work. This shows you items that you might like based on its experience of other shoppers' habits. This is a massive and very important area for anyone who has a product to sell. Big websites such as Amazon can afford to develop complicated algorithms that collect and crunch data automatically to bring you these results, but there is a growing number of ratings directories springing up – particularly if you work in the trades. Rated People is the top UK site for tradespeople, whether you're looking for someone to do some work or want to register as a trader yourself. TripAdvisor is another popular example, which lists hotels and holidays. It's worth looking around to find the right fit for your business, as you will be paying some kind of fee, usually for leads, to be listed in these directories. Always encourage happy customers to rate your delivery or fulfilment of the job. Ratings and comments are the currency of a site like this, so try to make every job count towards building your reputation. Although recommendation is a great way to ensure that you'll get quality work, in life or online, it's still not a guarantee. You should always check into the financial health of a company before making any significant payments up front (more on how to do that later in this book).

 TIP

Even in this age of digital everything and online automation, over 80% of consumers trust the recommendation of a friend over a written review. Try to persuade every happy customer who passes through your hands to post about you or share your pages with their networks, as this will be your most powerful route to new business.

BOOSTING YOUR VISIBILITY

Making it easier for customers to find you online

As I mentioned previously, most people search online when they want to find a local business. One billion names are searched for in Google every day and an astounding 94% of people never look beyond the first page of results. By following a few simple tips and presenting yourself as an expert on as many popular blogs and platforms as possible, you will see your company name rise steadily through the search results, the aim being to eventually arrive on that golden first search page. SEO is big business and we will barely graze the surface of it in the following paragraphs. There are many detailed and insightful books written on the topic, and plenty of agencies that will be only too pleased to help for a fee. But you don't need to spend a penny to get started along the path to online visibility. As Google is the most-used search engine by a long way, we will concentrate on ranking for this service.

www.google.com/webmasters/tools

Google uses an extremely complex software algorithm to calculate the relevance of your page to any given search query – but it has to find your page first. Bots, known as 'spiders', spend every waking second crawling across the web looking for new pages to index, but you can jump to the front of the queue by using Google's Webmaster tools. The full instructions for verifying that you own the site are reasonably complicated, but you should be able to follow them if you've already registered a domain name. Once it's been verified, you can use the 'Fetch as Google' tool under the 'Health' sidebar to request that a bot looks up your website. Once the message 'Fetch Status' stops flashing 'pending', the 'Submit to index' link will become clickable and you can use it to have Google add your page to the search directory. There are lots of other tools here that you might find useful for keeping an eye on the health, security and traffic stats of your site.

 TIP

www.google.com/webmasters/tools/submit-url
If you don't want to wrestle with Webmaster tools you can still submit a link to be indexed by Google, although your request may not be acted on very quickly. Just add 'submit-url' to the Google Webmaster tools address, and paste in the domain name that you want to include.

PAGE RANK IMPROVEMENTS

How to make your business more visible in Internet searches

If you want to rank highly for lots of popular search terms you're going to need professional help. The SEO industry is worth over £500 million in the UK alone, but if you just want to do well on a couple of search terms and your own company name, there are a few simple tricks that you can use to boost your page rank.

- **Include relevant key words:** when writing the text for your website, make sure that you include the kinds of key words and terms that potential customers might use to search for your products or services.
- **Linking:** your website's page rank will be heavily influenced by the number of 'links' leading both to and from it – so what about all those lovely communities and forums I was encouraging you to participate in earlier? Now's the time to make them pay dividends by ensuring that your web address is mentioned in every post you make. You can do this without being annoying by adding it to the way you sign off. Many community sites will let you set up an automatic 'signature' so that you will never forget to do this.
- **High-profile linking:** all links are good, but Google recognises certain websites as powerful influencers, such as popular blogs like Gizmodo, Mashable, Huffington Post and BuzzFeed. If your website is linked to or from one of their pages it could really fly up the rankings. We'll be looking at ways in which you can entice them into doing this later in the book.
- **Get a Google Plus social page:** even if you don't update it, it's worth having a presence on Google Plus with links to where you do hang out online, as it's been suggested that the Google search algorithm applies a greater degree of relevance to its own products in the page rankings – meaning that links are more likely to appear on the first page of search results.

brandyourself.com

Studies have shown that eight out 10 people in their twenties do a quick web search on a person before meeting them for a first date, so you can appreciate how common the practice must be in business. BrandYourself is a good place to get a boost when it comes to page ranking. The process is quite lengthy, so set aside a good half an hour to set up your account properly. You will then be stepped through creating a profile page specifically designed to add credibility to anything linking to and from it. Add 'positive' links about yourself to boost the effect. These can be the social pages we've already created, or anywhere someone has written about you. You can add only three links in the free account, and there are full instructions for 'boosting' the links, which makes the most meaningful connections possible as far as page-ranking algorithms are concerned. It could take a couple of weeks before you start to see solid results. Once people do start visiting your profile the service will let you know who they are, where they are located and how they found you, with more details available if you have a premium account.

THE SOCIAL WHEELS ARE ROLLING, ROLLING

You should now have all of the tools that you need to make the most out of the core social platforms, and pretty soon customers and potential customers will start joining you online. Keeping your nose clean and delivering interesting and relevant links and content are the only things you need to do in order to keep those social connections ticking over. Add to this the networks that you can start building with your peers online and in the physical world, and you are well on the way to being a truly 'connected business'. Increasing your visibility in search results and being included on recommendation platforms are key elements to getting the word out so that people can find you both on- and offline. SEO techniques take time to bed down before you start seeing big results, so just be patient and keep plugging away at the tips outlined in this chapter. Remember that you are competing for the first page of the search results with large companies that have the cash to pay for professional SEO services, so it will take time for your small business to chip away at their numbers. Quality over quantity is the way that you win this SEO battle, concentrating your efforts on techniques that will deliver the best results and building a strong personal relationship with your customers online to keep the competition at bay.

Chapter 3

Riding the cloud

Building an online community around
your business

So far we've covered a few basic activities that shouldn't take up
too much time, but there are even bigger rewards to reap if you
can spare a couple more hours a week. By creating and sharing your
own unique content not only do you start building a reputation as
an expert in your field and therefore a business to be trusted, but
as people share and recommend what you've made you'll find your
online networks growing organically in directions that you could never
have reached independently. In this chapter we'll be talking in more
detail about:

- why and how to blog for your business
- creating a narrative to engage your customers
- tools and platforms for podcasting, screencasting and video
  blogging
- building a simple website of your own
- finding those most interested in your work and encouraging
  them to recommend you to their own networks
- an interview with cowboy-turned-small-business evangelist
  Duncan Cheatle
- copyright issues and how to deal with infringement
- website analysis tools and how to use the data they
  produce.

BLOGGING IN THE CLOUD

Why and how to blog for your business

Having found your space on the web and begun gathering a crowd, the next natural step is to start engaging them. You can do this by creating interesting, unique content, stuff that they will want to link to and share with their friends, which will make sure that your name keeps bubbling up in the search rankings. On average, companies that run a regular blog experience 55% more web traffic than companies that don't, with more than half believing that they've taken on new customers directly because of the blog. Surprisingly, then, given those numbers, only 60% of companies actually do run a blog and more than half of those admit to not having updated it for over a year. It's not essential that you become a prolific blogger, but creating a new page every now and then that is optimised to help your performance in the search rankings can never be a bad thing. If business is a bit slow and you're just sitting there waiting for the phone to ring anyway, what have you got to lose? You might even uncover a hidden talent and become an Internet sensation! Maybe.

Bloggers now have so many ways to express themselves that it is getting ridiculous, and there are more than 133 million blogs (though, to be fair, the active bloggers I know all have more than one blog running, covering various different projects).

Twitter is a form of blogging platform, known as micro-blogging, though in reality it has evolved more into a highly effective noticeboard directing people to deeper content on the web. You can choose to blog the traditional way, using pictures and text, or you can make an audio blog, known as a podcast. You can screencast your desktop at the same time as recording your voice – a great way to create detailed 'how to' guides and step-by-step computer instructions if that is your line of work. Or you can go the whole hog and wow your audience with a video podcast, also known as a vlog (a contraction of video-blog). You can even blog with pure pictures if that's your thing – there are plenty of very popular photo-blogs and cartoon series if you look around. Pretty much anything goes these days in the blogosphere. It may seem far-fetched right now, but if you have the right idea, and do it in just the right way, at just the right time, you may be surprised at how quickly your link will spread. Remember, the more pages that link back to you, the higher your search engine ranking – and you might even catch a link from one of the blogging juggernauts like Mashable, if you're lucky.

Whatever medium you ultimately choose, there's a tool for you in this chapter, but we'll start with the basics and look at the good old-fashioned text blog. There are a lot of great free platforms if you're not going to be overloading your pages with high-resolution images; if your business is photography I suggest that you consider one of the premium upgrades to cater for your needs. All the platforms offer a nice range of templates that can be set up in minutes, but you can also go pretty deep with the customisation if you want to. Most offer some kind of analysis of your traffic, and we'll talk about how to use that when we cover analytics towards the end of this chapter. They almost all have some kind of smartphone app these days, so you can share thoughts the moment they occur to you. There are obviously possible downsides to this if you are in the habit of having 'brilliant thoughts' when you are out drinking with your friends!

You can write as much or as little as you want – just try to make it interesting or useful. Always remember who you're writing for. Post accompanying photos whenever you can – people do like a bit of eye candy – and put plenty of links to other sites throughout the text. Remember, the more pages linking to and from your blog post, the more credible it will look to those search engine bots, pushing your page rank upwards. You can add web addresses without it being annoying for your readers by using the 'insert hyperlink' option you can find in all the popular blog-posting tools. The icon usually looks like a three-ringed chain and lets you put a web address behind some words you've highlighted on your page. Readers will expect these links to lead somewhere relevant, and it's a great way to back up your words with source articles if you want to do some halfway decent journalism while you're at it.

TIP

Remember to try to use the key words that you want your business to be associated with in search results throughout the blog-post text, but make them relevant to what you're blogging about or you will be accused of 'key word loading' by your readers and they will most likely not bother to come back.

BLOGGING PLATFORMS

Popular websites for publishing your blog

www.blogger.com

Blogger is Google's own platform, so it will integrate nicely with your other Google properties. It's quick and uncomplicated – you can be up and blogging in just a few minutes after registration.

wordpress.com

WordPress is one of the long-standing web favourites for bloggers. Fast and unfussy, it has options for both beginner bloggers and those who want more control and customisation.

www.typepad.com

Typepad is another popular platform where it's quick to set up and get posting, with deep design customisation and all manner of plug-ins and extras if you want to get more involved.

www.tumblr.com

With its trendy, clean design, Tumblr has become known as *the* place to blog about anything visual, like art, photography or design. It would be a good place to post something like a step-by-step pictorial guide or photographic journal.

TIP

Complete 'key word' and other metadata boxes for every post. It's tedious, I know, but it's the whole point of posting unique content. Cut corners by creating a standard document with the key words you want to add every time – such as your company name and the selected search terms that you want to be associated with.

THE STORY CLOUD

Creating a narrative to engage your customers

If you're going to be consistent with your posting you should think about creating a narrative to get readers coming back. People love stories – and it doesn't have to be anything epic or fancy. Maybe you're renovating the lounge in a seaside guest house? Blog about your progress, including photos with a few words about how things are going, and you'll have regular guests itching to book a room to see it when it's finished. If you're providing local information or doing something interesting or worthy, such as running a marathon for charity, you can often get the local newspaper and radio stations to give your blog a mention, although you may end up having to be interviewed on the phone by an over-bubbly presenter at 7am – you have been warned! If you don't have enough time to build and feed an ongoing narrative on a stand-alone blog, there are plenty of fun alternatives to think about.

memolane.com

If you're already posting images and updates on the main social platforms and don't want to tie yourself down to doing a lot more work, Memolane lets you make attractive feeds, drawing content from all your social accounts to build an ongoing narrative around a particular topic. A feed can be shared or even embedded on a website or blog, and since it's constantly updated with whatever you are posting to Facebook, Twitter and the like, it will pretty much run itself. You can connect as many social accounts as you like, setting up different 'lanes' that filter content from your posts by certain key words. Individual posts can be excluded from the feed if you decide that you don't want to share them.

TIP

Never be too proud to ask family and friends for a leg-up by having them share your messages with their own social connections. If they live reasonably close by, this could be your most direct route to potential local customers.

storify.com

Storify recently took the social web by storm, offering a neat aggregation tool for gathering social comments, snippets of information and images from the web to tell an ongoing story. It has been used to great effect to capture cultural and sporting moments from a particular perspective, such as the London 2012 Olympics. If you're just starting out in business, why not begin a Storify to make a record of the way your company evolves? Even if you only ever share it with friends and family, they will probably all have social media accounts and may be willing to help you try to grow your business if they know what you're up to. Likewise, if you're running a competition or give-away, this can be a great way to let your customers track the entries and results. Stories are embeddable and SEO-friendly, meaning that the embed code has been optimised to work at improving your page rank.

TIP

Including your supporters' comments and links in your narrative will encourage more interaction, creating a positive feedback loop that should keep engagement levels nice and high. If no one is piping up, make a request for comments to be included.

www.inboundwriter.com

I hope you're beginning to see a pattern emerging that you don't actually have to spend much time doing stuff online, as long as everything you do has been optimised to improve your search visibility. I've given you a lot of techniques so far, but a relatively new platform, InboundWriter, takes some of the weight off bloggers' shoulders, as SEO checks are built into the architecture of the post-creation tool. This makes sure that you pay attention to the important SEO stuff, like working in those key words, even as the ideas tumble from your fingers.

From the outset you're asked to make choices and give information about what exactly you want to achieve. Be accurate and think carefully about what to tell it, as this information will be used to shape your optimisation and search the web for good examples of similar pages from which to draw inspiration. The results are never going to be perfect, so disregard any suggestions that are clearly out of whack. Even if you decide never to publish on the platform, just running through the sample document tutorial should help to solidify many of the SEO techniques we've spoken about so far.

The free account should be plenty for most casual bloggers, with the premium upgrades available if your project takes off.

CLOUD TALK

What is podcasting and how can you use it?

A podcast is just a radio show without a radio station; instead, recordings are usually downloaded to a portable digital player, such as an MP3 player or smartphone. Many high-budget TV and radio shows have a free podcast spin-off, so it's worth checking the iTunes directory for your favourite Radio 4 comedy or documentary series. People tend to subscribe to the podcasts that they enjoy, so new content gets downloaded to their devices automatically – rather like a magazine dropped through the front door. This can be a fun, effortless way to keep people informed about what's going on in your business. Even if you have no intention of recording your voice for public broadcast, you'll find lots of brilliant podcasts offering advice, discussion and opinion on countless specialist subjects, which can be really useful information for your own life and business.

audacity.sourceforge.net

If you do decide that you have something to say, the first step is to record it. Some podcasting tools let you record straight into the browser, though you tend to have less detailed control when editing and tweaking the sound. If you're going to take podcasting anywhere close to seriously, invest in a reasonably good-quality microphone and download Audacity, a free recording tool that lets you make professional-quality edits with whatever kind of quality finish you would like. To save your podcast as an MP3, the preferred format, you'll need to download and install the LAME MP3 encoder; search the Audacity 'Help' directory for simple instructions for doing this.

www.freesound.org

There are thousands of places where you can download free sound effects, usually in return for a mention when you use them. Freesound has never let me down so far when it comes to finding that quirky little sound effect that will add the finishing touch to a podcast episode.

 TIP

accidentaloutlaw.knowthenet.org.uk
Make sure that you don't fall into any copyright potholes by taking the quiz on this website. It could be an eye-opener in terms of what you are really allowed to do – and you may be surprised at how many times you would have broken the law otherwise.

POD PUBLISHING

How and where to share your podcast

You can publish your podcast right now, uploading it as an audio file to any regular blogging platform (including your Facebook page) for people to listen to through their browser. To truly be a podcast, though, it should be listed in the iTunes podcast directory. For this, your podcast needs to be saved as an MP3 file and hosted somewhere that offers an RSS feed. RSS is the main method used for collecting content from lots of different information streams, and any site that mass-syndicates content, like iTunes, generally uses RSS to automate the collection process. It's not actually very important for you to understand how RSS works in order to set up your podcast, though there are plenty of great articles online if you feel like Googling it.

You may find that a site you're already using includes an RSS feed – like Blogger and WordPress. If not, there are plenty of services designed for podcast hosting that offer a limited amount of storage space and bandwidth free of charge. It's important to understand the difference between 'Storage' and 'bandwith' before your podcast becomes popular. Storage is the physical space that your content will take up on the host company's server. This will vary depending on audio compression rates, but in general you'll need about 1MB per minute of recording; so a weekly half-hour show would need 30MB of storage per episode, giving you a monthly required storage total of 120MB. Bandwidth requirements are harder to predict as they depend entirely on your audience. With 100 subscribers enjoying your half-hour weekly show (each uses 120MB per month to download it), you would need 1,200MB (or around 12GB) of bandwidth per month to serve them.

www.podomatic.com

If you're looking for an RSS-friendly host that you can link to from the iTunes directory, PodOmatic is as good a pick as any right now, though you'd be wise to shop around for price and the best storage and bandwidth deals at the time of going ahead. Once your RSS feed is set up (which will be explained in the help section of any site that supports RSS feeds), use the URL that the podcast host gives you to 'Submit a Podcast' to iTunes. You do this by opening your iTunes Store and heading to the podcast page. You'll find the 'Submit a Podcast' link in the quick links panel to the top right of the iTunes screen. The whole process takes a few minutes and is very straightforward, but it may take Apple a few days to approve your podcast before it goes live. Once it does, though, every new episode that you put into your RSS feed will appear in the public iTunes directory and will be downloaded automatically to subscribers' mobile devices.

audioboo.fm

If you'd rather not think about all that technical stuff you can get started with Audioboo. It has a nice, clean online dashboard where you can record, edit, dress up and then broadcast your work of oratory genius. It's what you'd call maximum impact for minimum effort. There are smartphone apps for recording a 'Boo' on the go, which is a really nice way to interview people or perhaps report live on a local event. Once you publish a recording use the 'embed' feature to display it on your main social page or website, so that customers can easily find it.

TIP

Ask happy customers if they will record a quick Audioboo telling people how great you are, or what you did to impress them so much. This could make a fun collection of podcast entries, especially if you encounter any larger-than-life character. It would be very quick to put together and also make a nice collection of references to which you could refer potential clients.

SCREENCASTING THE CLOUD

Creating and sharing recordings of your computer screen

Whether you're making a guide to explain something to a large audience or want to deliver precise instructions to just one person, the next best thing to actually being there is a screencast. Screen-capture software lets you record the activity on your desktop and save it as an editable video file. You can record audio as well, so you can narrate whatever it is that you're showing on your screen. This could be 'how to use this website', or a slide show of the features of a new product— in fact, anything that can be visually illustrated on your computer. Screencasts are also excellent for teaching basic computer tasks to technically challenged relatives with bad memories!

You can publish your screencast through the same channels as a podcast – although you'll need to save the file as an .M4V (or other compatible) file if you want it to appear in iTunes. The thing to remember here is that video takes up a lot more storage and bandwidth than audio, so be careful that you don't start incurring costs.

TIP

Video file sizes vary widely, depending on the format used. MPEG-4 can average about 15MB a minute, where MS Windows' .AVI would be around 60MB. So a half-hour MPEG-4 video could be 450MB, which, to deliver weekly will require 1,800MB (or around 1.8GB) of bandwidth per month for every viewer.

www.screencast-o-matic.com

There are a few really good premium packages for recording your screencast, like CamStudio, which gives you lots of zoomy effects and nice, high-definition pictures. You can try most of these things for a limited period free of charge, but if you just want something quick and simple, check out Screencast-O-Matic. It is browser-based and records a 15-minute screencast that you can publish straight from the site or download to edit and polish before sharing. To make a longer show just record two 15-minute bits separately and stitch them together using a free video-editing package (coming up next). The free screen-capture program puts an unobtrusive watermark at the bottom of your recording.

 TIP

If you want to make the occasional screencast to share across lots of social networks and websites, YouTube is the quick and simple hosting option to make it accessible and easily embeddable on as many services and platforms as possible.

MOVING PICTURES

Video-editing tools and tips

Going in front of the camera for a video podcast is a brave move, and one that could gain you much notoriety for all the wrong reasons if you get it wrong. If you do decide to try to grab your 15 minutes of Internet fame, I strongly advise you to test your material on a friendly audience first, such as family and those friends who will be completely honest. How you record your material will depend on the hardware that you have available; for style ideas, check out the very many video podcasts (or vlogs) published on YouTube. Once you've figured out how to get your masterpiece recorded for posterity, here's a collection of tools you might find useful for editing it.

Windows Movie Maker

If you just want a quick and simple solution, Windows computers come with the perfectly adequate Windows Movie Maker installed as standard. Just fire her up, import your recordings and then drag and drop them onto the timeline. Add fancy transitions, titles and credits to jazz up your show, and finish with a soundtrack (but only if you have the rights to use it).

www.youtube.com/editor

If you're publishing on YouTube and just want to trim the top and tail off a recording, or bolt a couple of bits together, the site has its own simple, built-in editor that lets you add titles, captions and a music track as well – with a good selection of rights-free music tracks to choose from. These are songs that you can use free without breaking any copyright terms, which I'll explain in much more detail at the end of this chapter.

www.debugmode.com/wax

If you want a video editor that packs a bit more punch, Wax is a free download that will give you a lot more control over the finished product, but will take more time to master if you have no experience with video-editing packages. It looks a bit bare when you boot it up, but you'll soon fill those empty windows with multiple tracks, effects and transitions.

 TIP

The ultimate goal of all online marketers is 'going viral'. This is when you catch a trend and your creation gets picked up on a tidal wave of social sharing that reaches millions of people. You cannot plan to go viral – that's like trying to capture a breeze. To have a hope of going viral, your creation needs to be something that people want to share. Being funny and original will give you a fighting chance, but you'd better be ready for the bandwidth costs if you succeed.

HOME SWEET HOMEPAGE

Building a simple website

If you're still with me, congratulations – you are well on the way to controlling the Internet rather than having it control you. Setting up your own website, a place where you can bring all your online activity together into one place, serving up a unified, brand-optimised experience for the customer, is the natural next step. Through your own website you can sell products, deal with enquiries, list your services and share feedback from satisfied customers (perhaps embedding that 'satisfaction stream' podcast that I suggested earlier). Done right, it makes a really great shop window for your business and will drive you ever higher in the search results. You can write a regular blog, share photos and videos – most simple website editors let you embed Twitter and Facebook streams – and we've already covered several tools that let you make content to embed on other websites. Whatever you choose to include on your website, you need to focus on what it is that you want to achieve. Do you want people to 'like' you on Facebook so that you can be sure they see your marketing messages? Maybe you want them to request a quote or sign up for a newsletter? There should be a link or button on every page allowing visitors to easily fulfil that call to action. I'll bet you're thinking that it sounds like a lot of work. But if you want to get started quickly and with little fuss, there are some surprisingly versatile tools for creating professional websites using simple templates. These free tools may not make the most complex or robust websites if you're expecting heavy traffic, but for the purposes of starting to get your brand message out to the people who might be your customers, they make a perfectly capable website.

www.moonfruit.com

Moonfruit is a very easy site to use, with a great range of templates to suit most tastes. If your business is artistic there are some nice transitions and effects for displaying images in some of the templates. Once you've made your design choice you just click to replace all the place-holder images, videos and text with your own content (remembering to use those key search terms that you want to be associated with). The free account has a modest amount of storage, but certainly enough to start you off. If you're going to become a prolific web-page maker you may have to consider bumping your account up to one of the paid subscriptions. The site's templates are currently built using a technology called Flash, which is what gives you all the whizzy transitions. This can be a problem for some mobile platforms (mainly Apple devices), as it's a fairly old technology that isn't supported, so the site also offers a 'mobile build' option that lets you pull out key features to make a cut-down site suitable for mobile browsing in HTML5 (which is another, more universally supported website technology). Expect to see a lot more work and improvement from this company in using HTML5 templates in the future.

Keep your website storage needs down by hosting videos and images on free hosting platforms elsewhere – such as YouTube and ImageShack – and then simply embedding them into a page on your own website.

www.weebly.com

Weebly is another site builder with some snazzy free templates and a modest amount of storage and bandwidth free with the basic subscription. Like Moonfruit, right now it offers mainly Flash-based templates. One of its benefits if you're considering e-commerce is that you can run a small store from this platform – we'll talk more about that when we discuss how to earn money from your web presence in Chapter 10.

www.wix.com

Wix has many more comprehensive offerings in HTML5 templates for mobile and web browsers, so if you want your site to be accessible by anyone, anywhere, it's a great choice. It too is very simple to use and offers full e-commerce support if you want to open an online shop. The basic account is free, with premium upgrades and features if you want more tracking, analysis, bandwidth and storage space.

Plenty of websites will rent you a domain name if you want a personalised URL. Shop around for price on the extension you want – such as .co.uk or .com. The provider should have clear instructions on its website for how to set it up. Site-creation tools like the ones we have spoken about often let you buy a domain name from within the editor, making it super-easy to link the two together.

SPREADING THE WORD

Finding and informing a wider online audience

You have now fully arrived on the Internet, and it's time to start letting everybody know. You could go up to everyone's doors and push a flyer through the letterbox, but online you'll find more effective ways of getting the message out. Remember those 'social media influencers' that we discovered back in Chapter 2? The movers and shakers on Twitter and Facebook who engage with your posts and can reach a reasonable audience if they choose to share them? These are the people whom you should target with any new content that you post – but treat them with kid gloves and never let them feel that they are being 'sold' to. Also, comb through Facebook and LinkedIn groups to see if there are any niche communities that are a good match for you.

www.locafollow.com

We looked at Followerwonk in Chapter 2, but another way to dig around in Twitter looking for potential customers is with LocaFollow. You can drill down into area, biography text and even the content of a tweet. Results are sorted by number of followers, so you can see at a glance who is worth pursuing. Remember, if they are following as many people as follow them, it's highly likely that no one is reading anything they post, so you may as well not waste your time.

tweetlevel.edelman.com

Even a good 'follower to followed' ratio doesn't guarantee that the tweeter is being listened to, so run their Twitter name through the TweetLevel tool. It measures engagement, popularity and trust and comes up with an overall 'influence' rating. There are plenty of ratings tools popping up all over the web, and you shouldn't take their output as the only and gospel truth – but on the whole they should give you a fair impression of the general numbers.

bloglevel.edelman.com

If you have a new product or service to launch it can be worth targeting a few active bloggers to whom to send samples. If they like what you do, they may write about it on their blog – but be warned, they are equally likely to tell the world if they don't like what you do. Find the best bloggers to target with BlogLevel, a tool that lets you enter the web address of any blogs you are curious about to see which are the most influential.

Profile

Duncan Cheatle, Founder of the Prelude Group

"For most people the scarcest resource is time, so you need to make sure you're not wasting it by networking with the wrong groups."

Duncan Cheatle has had an unusual career, even working as a cowboy in the Brazilian outback in the 1980s. He's been championing UK enterprise for over 10 years, working with more than 1,000 entrepreneurs, and founded The Prelude Group to help fulfil his obsession to "make Britain the most enterprising nation in the world". He now heads up a number of successful ventures, including the award-winning The Supper Club, which is home to 260 of Britain's most exciting and high-growth entrepreneurs. At a minimum £1 million turnover, the membership criterion may be a bit rich for most new businesses, but you need to set the bar somewhere in order to build a group of similarly positioned entrepreneurs who can share real knowledge and insight when they meet; only then can a club at any level be truly successful. Duncan is also one of the co-founders of StartUp Britain, a private sector-funded campaigning organisation with the support of the UK government that promotes enterprise, and a director of the recently formed StartUp Loans company, chaired by James Caan of *Dragons' Den* fame.

Duncan said:

For most people the scarcest resource is time, so you need to make sure you're not wasting it by networking with the wrong groups. Find events for the sort of audience you want to mix with and decide why it is you're networking with them. It could be to generate business leads, or meet confidentially with your

peer group to gain knowledge and insight. It's a
waste of time to focus on the financial crisis too much,
especially if you're a small business or just starting up. The
broader macro-economic picture is largely irrelevant to these
companies, and in many ways a recession can work in your
favour; it may not be the easiest time to start out but you're
likely to build a strong business model and it forces you to focus
on the right things. Right now clients and customers are looking
for value and if you've got something that's a point of difference
then you probably have a better chance, or certainly as good
a chance as you did back in the 'good times'. The Internet has
made it significantly easier for a start-up to get going, reducing
capital costs to a fraction of what they were 15 years ago; you
can get online, communicate and reach audiences, seek out
knowledge, advice and content pretty much free, or at least at
very little cost. You can find customers all around the world in
a way that just wasn't possible 15 to 20 years ago. There is no
doubt the Internet has enabled pretty much anyone with the
get-up-and-go, the inclination and a reasonably good idea to
have a go at running their own business. So it's been a complete
game changer, but it's also important to remember to get out
and meet people or pick up the phone rather than sending an
email occasionally, because the personal touch and face-to-face
things are crucial too.

www.startupbritain.org

StartUp Britain has already launched many great, enterprising initiatives
that are really down to earth – from encouraging pub patrons to dream
up a business idea while they sup their pints, to providing a place to
search for start-up-friendly offices and co-working spaces in a particular
location. The latest project, StartUp High Street, finds empty or little-
used shops and encourages start-ups to get together in small groups
to take them over for a short time and make 'pop-up shops'. This not
only gives those start-ups a level of visibility they couldn't otherwise
have afforded but will also help to revive and rejuvenate the high street,
benefiting the broader economy as a whole.

www.facebook.com/StartUpLoansUK
StartUpLoans is one of the independent projects supported and promoted by StartUp Britain. Anyone aged 18 to 30 years old with a good idea can apply for a mentor-supported loan to start their business, getting valuable support and advice from established entrepreneurs as they formulate and then execute a business plan. It's run through a Facebook page, where they also post lots of great articles and ideas to help young people think more independently about their career paths.

COPYRIGHT QUERIES

Your intellectual property rights and how to protect them

If your original content starts attracting attention, you may worry from time to time about whether people are ripping you off. It is a sad fact of life online that your words, pictures and videos may one day get posted elsewhere without you receiving the appropriate (and legal) credit. You should try not to fret about it too much, because on the grand scale of things it's probably not going to impact on your business directly. If you want to guard against unauthorised use of your photos and videos, make sure that you set the copyright tags accordingly, wherever you store them. Sites such as Flickr and YouTube will always prompt you to do this during the upload process. For promotional content – in other words, content that you *want* people to share – choose one of the Creative Commons licence options. These detail a number of ways in which you can give other people permission to use your work for their own projects, provided they credit you as the source. Make sure that you put the copyright symbol '©' in the footer of all web pages too, to protect your text. Plagiarism is rife on the Internet, though things have improved greatly since Google added an element to its anti-spam algorithm that weeds out 'content farm' links. These were websites stuffed with text specially engineered to rank highly in search results. Words were churned out – often a direct copy-and-paste from elsewhere on the web – in the hope of snagging enough web traffic to earn some advertising bucks. But, since Google's changes were introduced in early 2012, that practice has pretty much gone away. Ultimately, you can't stop people stealing your content, but modern web tools have made it a lot easier to catch them at it.

www.google.com/alerts

Use Google Alerts to check if anyone is passing your words off as their own. Just pasting in a passage of not more than 32 words into the query box will show links to any pages on the Internet where that exact quote has been seen. You can also set up the query as an email alert so that you are notified as soon as Google finds it anywhere online.

 TIP

It's always good to know who is talking about you, so set up a Google Alert for your business or product name. It also makes sense to schedule an alert for the first line of your home postal address, as finding this on a page where it doesn't belong could be the first warning sign that your identity has been compromised.

---

www.tineye.com

TinEye is a reverse search engine designed to sniff out the origin of images on the web. Google image search does this too, but TinEye is a well-liked and efficient service and we've spoken about Google enough already, I think. Just upload your photo, or link to it on the web, and the service will use image recognition to see if the photo has been indexed anywhere else.

churnalism.com

If your business involves sending out press releases to the national and online media, Churnalism is an interesting site to bookmark. It scours UK press outlets for any article that has a high percentage of text copied word for word from any block of text that you paste into it. Some less-reputable journalists have been known to use lazy practices to fill their column inches, simply cutting and pasting large chunks directly from someone's marketing blurb. This site was designed to catch out 'churnalism' culprits, but it can also help you to keep tabs on the way your press releases are being used in the media.

COPYRIGHT THEFT

What to do if someone is stealing your content

If you catch an individual plagiarising your work, the best course of action is to write to them privately and politely, asking them to remove the material from their site immediately or fulfil the terms of your copyright licence. As we discussed earlier, public spats are never good for business, no matter how high the moral ground you're standing on. If they ignore or refuse your request, approach the website or blog host and explain the situation. All the major blogging and social platforms have very efficient customer service teams to deal with exactly this kind of issue and your complaint will always be taken seriously.

creativecommons.org

Creative Commons is a free licensing system that allows you to modify the copyright rules on creative work that belongs to you so that it is easier for other people to adapt and share it. Most major content-sharing platforms apply standard licensing terms when you upload anything so you don't have to worry about it. You can also use the free legal tools on the Creative Commons website to quickly and easily create your own custom licences that let people know very clearly what they can and cannot do with your content. This is especially important if you're uploading original content to your own website.

DON'T BE A COPYCAT

Copyright pitfalls to avoid when publishing content

Copyright is a two-way street and you should always respect the terms that other people have applied to their own creative works. If you can't see a copyright notice that doesn't mean that the work is not protected. If in doubt, send a message to the owner of the site seeking their approval to use their work. There are plenty of places online where you can find content that you are allowed to use, so there really isn't any need to cheat. You may come across graphics, software or materials that are labelled 'royalty-free' or 'copyright-free', but that doesn't always mean that you can copy or share them without authorisation. Make sure that you read the terms and conditions in any 'Click to Accept' agreements or 'Read Me' documents that come with the files, as these will normally detail the licence terms.

When posting photographs publicly make sure that you get permission from any people who are clearly identifiable in the image. It used to be enough to blur or pixilate their defining features, but image-recognition technology now makes it possible for a version of the photograph without the blurring to be found easily if it exists somewhere online.

If you receive a complaint, or a request to remove material that you have posted, take it down immediately. Even if you plan to dispute the claim, you are better off removing the material in question until the matter is resolved. The last thing you need is a copyright lawyer breathing down your neck.

COUNTING CROWDS

Website traffic-analysis tools and what the numbers mean

We've touched on the importance of using the data you collect about your followers to improve the way you interact with them – in other words, better results for less work (there is a theme developing here). The next few pages will delve a little deeper into analytics and cover some simple tools to help you make sense of all the numbers. People give away personal information on the web without even realising it, which is why it's important that you review the privacy settings of any network you join, so as to shore up your own defences. On most sites the default privacy settings are left pretty open – much to the concern of privacy campaigners – but public pressure has meant that your choices are becoming a lot more transparent and are easier to control. Sometimes it's good to give information to the web; it's what drives innovations like social recommendation and location searches, after all. Free traffic-analysis tools can tell you who is visiting your website or blog and which pages they liked best, allowing you to make more of what pleases them. We'll look at a couple of the most common tools in a moment, but first there are some technical terms that you need to understand.

COMMON WEB TRAFFIC-ANALYSIS TERMS

- **Page views:** each time someone arrives at your site and loads one of your pages it's counted as a page view, regardless of where they came from and where they go next, or if they have visited your site before.
- **Visits:** this counts the number of individuals visiting your website, regardless of whether they have been there before or how many pages they visit.
- **Unique visitors:** this is the important number for measuring your reach, as it counts only the first-time visitors during the period (day/month) when they land on one of your pages. This gives you the truest number of individuals visiting your site.
- **Pages/visits:** this figure tells you how many pages people visited each time they came to your website. Since you want to create 'sticky content' that gets people delving deeper, the higher this number the better.
- **Average visit duration:** the average time spent on a company website is usually under 5 minutes, and, again, the higher this number the better. Facebook actually bucks the trend, with the average time spent on the site by users being around 20 minutes per session – one of the reasons why it's such a powerful marketing platform.
- **Percentage new visits:** this is an interesting statistic if you want to know how good your social outreach is, as it measures the number of people arriving on your pages who have never visited you before.
- **Bounce rate:** this shows the percentage of people who arrived on your website and jumped straight off again, which could indicate that they didn't find what they were looking for or arrived there by mistake. This number should be as low as possible, but the average bounce rate is around 50%, so don't be too alarmed if yours hovers around that mark.

www.google.com/analytics

Google Analytics has pretty much become the standard tool that most website developers use to gather and analyse data about their visitors, and all the social platforms that count have some level of analytics built in. If you're setting it up on a website or blog, you'll need to open an account with Google Analytics and then add all the online assets you want to keep track of. You'll get a snippet of code to add to your web pages that will give the analytics program permission to gather visitor statistics. For many of the website- and blog-creation tools we've already looked at there will be a section in the control panel dedicated to setting up Google Analytics, so just follow the instructions and it should be fairly straightforward. Once Analytics is in place, give it a few days for some data to be collected and then take a look at your dashboard to see what's been happening on your website.

 TIP

The 'real-time' update panel tells you who's on what pages right now. If you have just fired off a mass-marketing message or an event is coming to a climax, keeping a watch on this number could provide valuable insight as to which promotional platforms are most effective.

getclicky.com

Another provider of analytics data is Clicky, which can also display information about what web pages your visitors arrived from, and even where they are based. With this knowledge you can fine-tune your promotional activities, concentrating on what works best. Once you've registered, you'll get a snippet of code to add to your pages. Check under the 'Apps and Plugins' link to see if they have integration with the publishing platforms that you use, as a lot of popular sites are covered. Click the link for full instructions on how to add your code to your own blogging site. With the free account you can track one website with a maximum of 3,000 daily page views, which should be plenty when you're just starting off.

woobox.com/statichtml

Facebook Insights is a free analytics dashboard you get when you set up a brand page, but the information is pretty limited. By installing the 'Static HTML Tab' feature that you can find for free at Woobox, you can add tabs to your Facebook brand page that let you include HTML, which is basically what that snippet of code is that's being bandied about by sites like Clicky. Add the 'tabs' feature, then launch it on your Facebook page to authorise it. You can now add extra tabs for all sorts of reasons, but if you sign up with Clicky using your brand page as your specified website – for example, Facebook.com/WorkingTheCloud – you can add the code that it generates to the HTML box on your shiny new tab to start tracking visitors to your brand page.

www.google.com/trends

There's no point in creating lots of unique content if no one is interested in it. You can find out what's got people curious on the web by using the Google Trends search tool. It lets you build a complex query, including location or time ranges, to find out what key words people are searching for the most. It can help you to pick out an emerging trend in an area that you can contribute to, giving your content the best possible chance of catching the public's eye.

www.campalyst.com/plugin

Earlier in this chapter we talked about targeting key influencers to help spread the word about your business. Campalyst Tweet Lookup Plugin is a simple tool that tells you who is directing the most traffic to your website, so you can see at a stroke who to keep on your free samples and promotion list. You need to be using Google Analytics on the website in question, then just authorise this tool and it will mail a full report to you when it's been compiled.

klout.com

There are a lot of websites and services claiming to deliver the 'definitive social influence score' across a range of popular networks. For the most part these are designed as fun trivia with no solid 'science' behind the scores and you shouldn't base any major business decisions on this data alone. But they can be a good barometer to give you an indication of how you're doing without too much effort on your part. Klout is probably the most famous of these. It lets you connect the popular content-sharing and social sites, whether your thing is words, pictures, videos or sharing your location. With an overall influence score compiled out of all your activity and follower interactions, the statistics for each connected service are also tracked separately for the last 90 days. It makes for a great all-round snapshot of whether your social standing is on the way up or sliding back down. It will also pick out your top influencers for you, so you will know at a glance who is doing the most sharing on your behalf and perhaps deserves a little more attention.

TIP

Search for your competitors' social accounts and Klout will reveal the most influential people who are engaging with them. These people would make a good target for your own marketing activities, though be careful not to anger them by sending repeated marketing messages, or you could find your account blocked and reported for spam.

A MEASURE OF YOUR SUCCESS

You should now be starting to see some real and significant value in spending a few hours each week dedicated to producing original content and maintaining your social connections. Making sure that you're not wasting time chasing after phantom leads or people with little or no social reach to benefit your business will really help you to streamline operations so that you get the best value for the time you spend online. As your reputation and audience grow, your SEO score will gradually improve, pushing you up the search results so that more people can find you, so be sure to pay attention to the details like tagging and key word placement in everything you publish. Nurturing relationships with brand influencers is really important, as there is plenty of competition for your customers' attention. Never forget that there is a human being at the end of any Internet exchange, and you are likely to be treated with respect in return.

Chapter 4

The essential web

A belt-and-braces tour of the web if you want
a connected business

By now your website is up and running; you're posting regular updates
on your blog or social pages; your key influencers are getting everyone
talking about you; and your reach and reputation are growing steadily.
That's quite a lot, considering we're not even halfway through this
book, but the Internet isn't just about social media marketing (you can
breathe a sigh of relief now). Facebook has been around only since
2004, and Twitter is younger still; but from the moment the World
Wide Web officially opened its doors to the public just over 20 years
ago, people have been filling it up with an astonishing collection of
some of the most ingenious stuff that humanity has ever seen. In this
chapter we'll be taking a look at the amazing services and downloads
that can benefit any business, any size, based anywhere in the world.
This chapter covers:

- complete office management suites
- team resources and task managers
- productivity tools to help you get things done
- collaboration and file-sharing tools
- data storage and backup services
- online recruitment and job-finding tools
- interview with Rajeeb Dey, one of the UK's most successful
  young business people
- contact management tools and tips.

CLOUD ESSENTIALS

Tools and resources for everyday business

Google has now recorded over 8.4 billion pages on the World Wide Web, and that figure rises to 17 billion and beyond when you estimate the number of pages that haven't yet been indexed by any search engines; and that's just child's play when you look at smartphone apps, which are predicted to reach over 76 billion downloads by 2014. Yes, I did say 76 billion. You can find a tool online in the app store to fulfil pretty much any business function you could want, if you know where to look (or if you know of a good book that does!). There is some pretty obscure stuff out there, and we'll go off on various interesting tangents throughout the remaining chapters, but for now I want to cover a few basic essentials that may get you thinking more like a connected business. A lot of the mundane office and administrative tasks that you have to handle every day can be stored and dealt with in the cloud, giving you and all of your staff easy access wherever they are, and whatever device they are using to connect to the Internet. It's amazing how much more productive you can be when all the spokes are connected to a single online hub; and a lot of the services we'll be exploring have plenty of automation features, turning a tortuous all-day administrative task into a couple of clicks, and you're away.

 TIP

The term 'syncing' is used to describe the process of all your data being updated across all your online locations, for everyone attached to your network – and it's a term you'll see a lot when looking at any decent cloud service.

THE CLOUD OFFICE

Complete business solutions for managing a team online

If you're starting a business from scratch or planning a major overhaul there are several good management tools that you can use to help things go more smoothly. Whether you're running a team or working solo there are real benefits to storing office essentials in the cloud. First, you can access your data from anywhere, which is useful if you're out and about a lot, as you can hop onto a free WiFi network in a coffee shop and find everything that you'd usually have at home. If you work in a team there are huge benefits, allowing you to share and collaborate on projects with colleagues, and even to plan and schedule the workload. Connected teams don't need to live close to each other, so you can open up your search for talented staff. These days you can build a dream team across scattered locations and have as many meetings, chats and water-cooler moments as your physical-world counterparts do, the only difference being that you don't have the massive overheads of running an office building.

www.planetsoho.com

At SohoOS you'll find everything you need to process orders on a single dashboard that is clean and uncomplicated. On the right, you access sections covering estimates, invoices, stock, purchase orders and general office documents. The 'Timer Tracker' feature lets you manage multiple client timesheets and billable hours, but this is a premium upgrade option, along with several other useful features. There is nothing fancy about the free tools in this suite but they do the job quite adequately, and once you've set up a system the paper trail links seamlessly together through your online hub. Buying stock, keeping track of it and eventually selling it to your customers can be done with just a few simple clicks. You get a very basic business page – we've looked at far better tools for this already – but it's worth filling it out and adding it as another link to your website, and it might just lead the occasional customer to you through a random web query. It's also worth taking a look at the website's blog, as it posts regular and very helpful tips and articles to help you run your small business more effectively.

 TIP

You can often sign in to web-based services using your Facebook, Twitter or other social accounts. Offering this option is a growing practice amongst website developers, known as 'social logins'. Not only does it mean that you have few or no further details to add in order to complete your registration, but sharing options are also nicely integrated for future use.

skylightit.com

Running a chaotic team can be like herding cats, but thankfully there are plenty of tools online to help you throw a net of productivity over them. We'll be looking more specifically at creative collaboration tools in Chapter 9, but Skylight is a good all-rounder if you have a project or team to manage and want a central command station. You can assign and track tasks for multiple projects, manage everyone's calendar, billing and budgets, upload files to share, and keep an eye on resources. There's even a messaging system and shared contacts database, so no more bothering each other for Mr So-and-so's mobile number. A nice, succinct introductory video when you first launch your browser will get you up and running swiftly. The free account has limited storage and handles only two projects with two collaborators, with paid upgrades for more people, projects and storage space.

 TIP

Collaboration platforms like this can be the perfect place to start working seriously on a business plan without having to meet up constantly. Seeing each other tick tasks off the to-do list can also really drive momentum, and if you suspect that somebody isn't pulling their weight it will be plain for all to see.

TO DO, OR NOT TO DO

Productivity tools to help you get things done

I've always been a big fan of lists; it's pretty much the only way I can keep on top of all the tasks involved in running my day-to-day business. Time is a precious commodity and there are dozens of productivity tools and to-do-list managers to help you save more of it, offering whatever level of detail or control you personally feel comfortable with. We're going to be looking at more time-saving tools in Chapter 7 when we explore how your virtual assistant can take the pressure off your workload, but for now I have a few solid suggestions to help manage your team's task list more effectively.

iqtell.com

This site is a newcomer to the field, but is linked to the 'Getting Things Done' (GTD) brand, which has gained a lot of traction in productivity circles in recent years. As well as providing lots of apps, tools and storage for completing day-to-day office chores, it has all the GTD productivity features integrated with the dashboard, so you won't even notice how organised you are until you're sitting at your desk wondering what to do next. There are mobile smartphone apps and the registration process steps you through, adding popular email providers, which is handy for managing your email through a single dashboard if you have more than one account. There is a lot you can do with this package, so it's worth taking a look at the tutorials, which you'll find under 'IQTELL Tours' when you click the little 'gear' icon next to your login details in the top right-hand corner of the main dashboard. At the time of writing this service is still in private beta, which is an 'unfinished' version of the software distributed to a limited group of users for testing and feedback. The site will be live to the public by the time you read this, but you'll have to check the pricing structure and storage limits, as those details haven't been released yet. That said, the developers have told me that there is likely to be a free account with cut-down features and limited storage, with the upgrade to premium features and "no storage limitations" costing "a few dollars a month".

www.wunderlist.com

Wunderlist is another great option that lets you manage all your tasks through a central dashboard that supports most computer and mobile platforms. The layout is a little less formal than the other tools we've looked at and there are some neat social features that let you share a list publicly through the 'CloudApp' feature. This will tie in very nicely if you're looking forward to learning about how you can get extra funding for your business through the social web – otherwise known as crowdfunding, which we'll cover fully in Chapter 10.

tracky.com

Tracky takes the social web and gives it another twist, providing a to-do list platform where you can track conversations and build a network from your contacts to collaborate on specific projects. This is productivity tooled down to the bare minimum, so it should suit those who just want a quick and easy way to be more organised.

basecamp.com

At the other end of the spectrum, Basecamp is very business-like and formal. One of the longest-standing and most popular team collaboration platforms, it's not free, although you do get a good 45-day trial to decide if you want to start paying monthly. It contains everything you could need to run team projects from the cloud. Because it's been around so long there are also quite a few useful third-party applications that integrate with it seamlessly, which can be a big time-saver if you really take to the cloud. We may even come across one or two of these applications in the chapters to come, so keep your eyes peeled if you have to manage a team.

SHARING THE CLOUD

File-transfer services for sharing data with colleagues

Once you've set up your office in the cloud you're going to start needing to share things: documents, contracts, graphics, video, and depending on your line of work that could all add up quite quickly. Today almost 625 terabytes of data are transferred across the Internet every 60 seconds (that's 625 trillion MB, if you're interested), and with the number of connected devices forecast to reach two for every human being on the planet by 2015, the information superhighway is going to get more and more crowded every day. To make sure that your data gets where it needs to be, I've picked out a filing cabinet full of great ways to save and share various different file types.

www.wetransfer.com

If you have a large file to deliver to a single recipient, WeTransfer lets you send one, or a collection of files, up to 2GB in total. There's no sign-up needed and when the file is uploaded it will email you a link that you can share with more people. You'll also be notified by email when the file has been downloaded. Sending files this way means that they are stored online for the recipients to download at a time that is convenient for them, rather than them trying to pick up a 2GB attachment when they are out on a mobile connection – which will not make you very popular at all. While your files are uploading, the website's background image changes constantly, so it looks rather pretty while it's working too.

www.justbeamit.com

Another way to send files up to 2GB in size, JustBeamIt lets you set up a direct link to another person's computer to funnel the data through. The technology is known as a peer-to-peer service — you may recognise the name from reports about pirated music, movies and software. This service is both completely legal and very simple to use. Just tell it which file you want to send, and you'll get a link that you can give to whomever you want to be able to download it. You can send this link by email, SMS, instant message, whatever you like; the key here is that you must leave your computer turned on with JustBeamIt active until the person you are contacting has opened the link and downloaded the file straight from your machine. The download is free and the service is very secure, as you are sending the file person to person, without it passing through anybody else's server.

imagevat.com

For images that you want to post in blogs or share through your social channels, Imagevat is a fuss-free solution. No sign-up, just choose a picture and away you go. There is no option to make images private but you can note copyright details in the comments, as well as contact details for more information. Once the image is uploaded you get a link and various embed codes to use around the web. The service offers unlimited web space and bandwidth — which could prove very handy if your image becomes an Internet sensation and is viewed by millions of people.

 TIP

Uploading images and videos to external content-hosting sites and then embedding them on your own website or blog means that everyone who views the content will be eating away at the host's data bandwidth rather than your own.

www.dropbox.com

Dropbox is a storage solution that connects a folder on your desktop to some space in the cloud. This is incredibly useful if you work across several computers in different locations, as you can install the app on any machine and link it up to your folder. You can share folders with collaborators, making it the perfect online filing cabinet, and any changes made to files are synced immediately, right across the web. Dropbox also has the benefit of being a veteran in what is becoming an ever more crowded space, so you'll find a few useful business tools that have Dropbox integration – as we'll see in the next few chapters. You get 2GB of free storage, going up to 16GB by referring friends. It's available for Mac and PC with Android, Apple and BlackBerry smartphones covered – and for $10 a month you can upgrade to 50GB of storage. If you're going to be sharing your folders with other people, there are a couple of useful monitoring tools that you should make use of.

- dropbox.com/account is a web page where you can see exactly which computers and mobile devices are linked to your account.
- If you head to dropbox.com/events you'll be able to track all the recent activity within your folders.

 TIP

You can make your Dropbox account even safer by activating the 'two-step verification feature', either by downloading the smartphone authentication app or by submitting your mobile number in order to receive a temporary access code when you want to log on. Lots of data storage sites now offer this feature, including Google, and you'd be wise to activate it wherever possible, as it means that intruders would need more than just your password in order to steal your data.

www.zumocast.com

ZumoCast is a free download for Windows, Mac and Linux machines that turns your computer into a peer-to-peer server, letting you transfer or stream media instantly without the need to upload or synchronise files to any online drives. It effectively turns your home computer into a cloud drive, though your machine must be fired up and working properly for you to access it remotely. As well as being able to transfer files, you can stream all your music and video, which is scanned and referenced by the software when you first install it. To top it all, free apps for Android and Apple mobile devices mean that you can hook into your files and media on the move – although be aware of data costs when streaming music and video over a mobile network, which can be very expensive.

minus.com

Sometimes you'll want to share files with a group of people, or give people a choice of photos or images. Rather than pushing all the information out to everyone, use Minus to set up an online stash box so that invited users can review the posts and download only the content they need. As well as for team work, this is a great way for families to share photographs from a wedding or big celebration. The 'drag and drop' interface, which lets you drag file icons with your mouse pointer and just 'drop' them into the website's upload box, makes adding files quick and easy, even for a novice. With a desktop app available for Windows, Mac and Linux, mobile apps for Apple and Android, plus a whopping 50GB of free storage to start you off, this has to be high on the list of essential online team resources.

BACKUP BUDDY

Online backup services and data storage

It's a sad fact of life that the first time most computer users will think about backing up their data is just after they have lost everything in a drive failure or other deadly digital occurrence. These are thankfully rare, but they can happen – as I learnt to my despair when a factory reset tried to install itself onto my connected external hard drive (where I had 'cunningly' stored all my working documents to keep them safe from system crashes – doh!). Luckily the damage was limited, as I have always been in the habit of backing up 'every so often'; I now make sure I auto-backup to a remote location at the end of every day. The cost is negligible in time and money and it means that I will never lose two months' writing again. Extensive studies have recently shown that only 10% of all computer users back up their data daily and, shockingly, nearly a third of people have never backed up anything at all. Ever. I don't have to tell you what a bad idea this is – and if you're sitting there feeling a bit sheepish because you're one of the careless third, listen up, because by the end of this section you should never have to worry about data loss again. There are loads of free options for backing up your files, with more popping up all the time as cloud computing grows. I've picked out a few of the front runners to give you an impression of what's out there today, but in this fast-moving space you should definitely check to see which new services offer the best current prices for the storage and features you want.

www.backblaze.com

Backblaze is an easy solution for PC and Mac that continuously saves what you select – from a single file to the whole hard drive. Data is heavily encrypted, and in the case of a total wipe-out you can download your data as a compressed folder from which your computer will extract everything automatically, or you can order a USB drive to be posted to you. You can try the unlimited service for 15 days, after which there's a monthly subscription of around $5.

www.crashplan.com

CrashPlan is an interesting service that lets you back up free to another 'always on' computer, either in your home or, if you have a friend with excess hard drive space, elsewhere (as long as you trust them with all of your data!). It is available for Mac, Windows and Linux and there are also well-priced unlimited storage space plans if you don't know anyone with drive space to spare.

www.sugarsync.com

SugarSync is worth a mention, as it lets you back up any folder on your computer, syncing it everywhere you work in real time. It also includes apps for Windows Phone 7, Symbian and the Kindle Fire – and with 5GB free storage to start you off, this is good competition for Dropbox.

drive.google.com

Google Drive may be the new kid on the backup block, but integration with Google's other cloud offerings makes this a good pick for sharers and collaborators. There are free apps for Android and Apple mobiles. You get 5GB of free storage, with competitive pricing for upgrades.

skydrive.live.com

Not to be outdone by its main webmail rival, Microsoft also has a cloud drive service that links to your Hotmail or online Outlook address and lets you share folders with other accounts. At the time of writing this offers the best deal in terms of storage cost, with 7GB free and just £32 a year to upgrade to 100GB. There are downloads for desktop access on PC and Mac and smartphone apps for Apple, Android and, of course, Windows mobile devices. Your data can be accessed any time without a download through the browser interface, which is handy if you're working in a public space.

www.cloudfogger.com

Security should always be a priority where your company's data is concerned. Cloudfogger adds an extra layer by encrypting your data to a standard approved by the US National Security Agency for top secret information. Once you've selected a folder to encrypt, you can still view and open files inside it with ease, but if anyone breaks in they will just see a jumbled mess. Integration with leading services like Dropbox and Google Drive means that you can apply this encryption to your cloud storage space if you like. If that space is a shared folder you don't even need to give your encryption details to invited collaborators, as they will also be able to open the files if you've authorised sharing the folder with them.

socialsafe.net

One last tool that you may appreciate if you start making meaningful connections on the social web is SocialSafe. This is a backup tool for all those vital social accounts and messages, so that you will never lose track of an influencer. The free version will let you see what the service is about, backing up limited data from just one Facebook profile. The enterprise version involves a modest annual subscription to unlock the real power of this tool, as you can save everything from 10 Facebook pages and profiles, as well as many other leading sites like Twitter, Google Plus, LinkedIn, Instagram and more. This service extracts your data to be stored somewhere that you specify, so you are limited in storage space only by what you have available, either on your hard drive or on another online space, such as Dropbox.

TIP

www.worldbackupday.com
The date 31 March has been designated 'World Backup Day'. I'm not quite sure who has the authority to sanction such control over the calendar, but the website to support the event has a great and ever-growing collection of the latest tools and developments in the world of data backup, and so is well worth a visit every now and then.

FIND YOUR CROWD IN THE CLOUD

Recruitment services and job-finding tools and resources

Most growing businesses will need to take on new staff eventually, and here the social web is having another massive impact. The online recruitment market has enjoyed a growth curve linked to the rise of the social web, as this is the perfect place to make connections and mingle with potential colleagues. One of the reasons why the huge social giants (like Facebook, LinkedIn and Twitter) have become such a roaring success is that they have opened up the doors to the inner workings of their website to independent developers so that they can program their own unique and handy features for users. Like so many other emerging hot trends, recruitment networks have really capitalised on this, providing some ingenious services to connect workers with jobs.

www.twitjobsearch.com

Most companies with a social presence now routinely tweet any vacancies they have, and a growing number of job seekers are heading to TwitJobSearch to find them. The website scours around 50 million tweets a day looking for vacancies that are being advertised. By drilling down to location and key word people can search for relevant jobs, with new posts popping up in real time. If you're looking for staff it's worth listing your vacancies here, but you can also check for any freelance or contract work that may be available if that's the kind of business you're in.

workaround.me

Location search has been a game changer for many sectors, and recruitment is no exception. Smartphone apps let people look for work wherever they are standing – ideal for casual workers looking for part-time or temporary employment. WorkAround.me has a free iPhone app for job seekers to download and look for any work registered around them. If you own a shop or cafe and need some last-minute cover for a sick employee or a runaway promotion, you can jump onto the site and add your vacancy to the database, setting a start and finish date and an hourly rate, as well as details about the role. With no registration or payment required, the service will add your job to its mobile app, so that anyone searching close by can find you. It's not as massively populated as somewhere like Twitter, but it's still a fairly new platform and there is already a good crowd building. You may just strike it lucky if you advertise here; it won't cost you anything, after all.

www.gild.com

There are endless niche networks if your needs are more specific, like Gild, which attempts to 'gamify' finding an advanced technical job. 'Gamification' is a rather pretentious buzzword that's been adopted to mean making a task more fun. Developers gamify a process by presenting its elements as a challenge – in the case of Gild, they've made showing off your experience into a competitive game with a series of quizzes and programming challenges where only the most skilled candidates will score highly. This would be an excellent place to find a web developer who genuinely knows how to code, for example, as they will have had to prove it in order to rank well on the site.

www.simplicant.com

If you're hiring a lot of new people you should probably think about drafting in some virtual help to keep track of the applications. Simplicant lets you keep track of all interesting candidates' CVs in one place, linking to Facebook, Twitter and LinkedIn to make networking with potential employees really easy. You can also connect with your existing contacts, seeking references and referrals as well as getting help with spreading the news about your jobs. If the service works for you, after 15 days you'll have to pay a monthly subscription starting at $40 to manage two open positions.

☕ *TIP*

Use jobs boards to scout for freelance and contract opportunities. If you see a job being advertised in your line of work, don't be afraid to approach the company and suggest that they consider hiring you on a contract basis – you don't have anything to lose, and if you convince them you will be first in line for the work.

Profile

Rajeeb Dey, Founder of Enternships.com

"The key is to make sure you have the right team around you, and if you feel you don't have all the necessary skills or expertise, find others who complement you when setting up your business."

At 26 years old, Rajeeb Dey is one of the UK's most high-profile and successful young business people. Like so many web entrepreneurs, he came up with the idea for his business while still studying at university, where he was the president of Oxford Entrepreneurs, one of the largest student entrepreneurial societies in Europe. Giving the 'internship' model a good shake-up, Enternships is a web service that connects young people with work experience placements in start-up organisations and SMEs. The company has so far connected more than 4,000 businesses in over 20 countries with graduate talent, including companies such as Groupon and PayPal. He is also one of the co-founders of StartUp Britain, won the O2 Young Entrepreneur of the Year award in 2009 and was named one of 2012's Young Global Leaders at the World Economic Forum. Not a bad record, considering that he finished university only in 2008. So what is the secret of such rapid success?

Rajeeb said:

I started Enternships.com whilst still studying, as a very basic listings site for Oxford University students to find opportunities in small companies. But when I graduated in 2008, in the midst of an unemployment crisis, it became clear there was a gap in the market. If you can make your business relevant to current events and show how it meets a pressing need, it has a much better chance of success and you are more likely to grab the attention of the media. The barriers to entry for businesses on the Internet are very low, so it's important that you find a way of rising above the bubble and making yourself stand out. You need to get people talking about you, so with Enternships I created a new word – a contraction of 'entrepreneurial internships' – with the aim of creating a culture change where work placements are based in a much more entrepreneurial environment than the traditional blue-chip corporation. It's also important that you can scale an online business quite quickly, creating enough barriers around you to stand up against the competition. I didn't originally plan for Enternships to become a company, so I didn't take the time to find the right team around me. Not being from a technical background I struggled a bit with getting the website set up and working with contractors, costing valuable time and money. If I did it all over again I would invest in finding myself a co-founder who had the ability to build and manage the website whilst I focused on my strengths of marketing, business development and sales. The key is to make sure you have the right team around you, and if you feel you don't have all the necessary skills or expertise yourself, find others who complement you when setting up your business.

www.enternships.com

You can sign up as a candidate or an employer. Candidate membership is free, but for companies looking to advertise a vacancy it's a lot like placing a traditional advert and you're going to have to pay. There are a couple of listings options that you can check out under 'Pricing'. The enhanced listing will give you much more exposure through the site's social media activity, so it might be worth thinking about upgrading if you hope to fill a key position.

CROWD CONTROL

Tools for managing information about the people you meet

I think most people have trouble remembering faces when they meet a lot of them, so it's useful to have some kind of contact management system set up right from the start. You never know when you might need the advice or input of an expert you've met at some point in the past – but which drawer did you stuff their business card into? Most phones now have detailed address book options built in (provided that you remembered to enter the details), but if you want more control and flexibility in how to access them there are plenty of great, free cloud services to record and store all of your interactions. Some even let you add context about how, why and where you met, which could be very handy for finding your way back to their offices in the future.

www.cardcloud.com

Cardcloud is a free app for Android and Apple mobiles that acts as a virtual business card that you can swap with other users. If your contact doesn't want the Cardcloud app, you can send your information via email or through the mobile site. In this instance their details can be entered into your contacts list by hand, using the location marker and comments to add important context about where and why you met. This information is also available through the browser-based dashboard and on any mobile device.

TIP

When setting up new contact management tools, never give your clients' email addresses to a provider for them to be invited. Some of these services are quite aggressive with their follow-up email policy, and if someone doesn't want to register it can become very annoying for them, being spammed with reminders about your invitation forever more.

rapportive.com

With Google's Gmail being such a widely used service, there are oodles of great browser add-ons that give you a more personalised and streamlined email experience. Add-ons are quick and easy to install, as they just make a tweak to an existing program – in the case of Rapportive, that's your online email interface when viewed in Firefox or Chrome browsers. This plug-in joins up all the dots by letting you see your Gmail contacts' social connections, pulling up a photo, location and job description beside every incoming message. You can widen your network by connecting Facebook, Twitter and LinkedIn accounts; you can even keep notes, perhaps warning a 'future you' about a bad exchange you had with a person, or if they were slow to settle your invoice. When additional information is available through the social streams, the app will report on recent posts, blogs and other network activity. This could be an excellent way to run a quick check on a potential employee to make sure that their behaviour is appropriate.

www.soocial.com

One of the downsides of having so many ways to connect with the world is it can be easy to fragment your contacts list across multiple devices and online sources. Soocial lets you sync all these up into one safe, searchable storage vault. The free account syncs from three sources (including Gmail, Outlook, Windows Live and most smartphones) to a maximum of 250 contacts, after which there is a small monthly subscription for a premium account (which you can try free for 30 days when you first register). Make sure you carefully read all the warnings

TIP

As we uncover more browser add-ons, also known as extensions or plug-ins, later in these chapters, you'll hear a lot about the combination Chrome/Firefox being supported by developers. This is due to these platforms becoming the best browsers of choice for feature-rich and enhanced web surfing.

and instructions when connecting each source as it will save you a lot of time backtracking later if you miss an important detail.

CLEAR AS CLOUD

The fog should be lifting a little now

You should now be pretty clued up about how to run your business in the cloud, with essential tasks and scattered team members coming together seamlessly under one virtual roof. Far from you spending hours slaving over a hot computer, the productivity tools and essential services in this chapter should help to streamline your activity, giving you more time to concentrate on drumming up new business while the Internet takes care of the rest. With your data safely backed up somewhere in the cloud, even the most devastating setback can be recovered from in hours; and if you make use of one of the many great contact management services you need never lose touch with any important contacts – or worse, forget who they are when you bump into them socially.

Chapter 5

Why pay full price?

Free alternatives to essential
business software

Take a look around your computer and you'll probably find it stuffed
to the top of your monitor with brand-name software that is pretty
much essential to your everyday business life. Microsoft Word, Excel,
Photoshop, even the operating system itself is likely to be Windows or
Mac. This lot either set you back several hundred quid (even if it was
bundled into the price of a new computer, you're still paying for it), or
you bootlegged it from a pirate site, in which case you're not getting any
support (and, by the way, you are breaking the law). But it doesn't have
to be this way. There are loads of 'open source' and free alternatives to
office essentials; and these days they are every bit as easy to use as their
expensive commercial cousins. In this chapter we'll be covering:

- the 'open source' software movement making applications free
- free alternatives to essential applications
- an interview with Tony Banks, Falkland's war veteran and a
  Channel 4 'Secret Millionaire'
- the best cloud solutions for your digital communication
- tools for editing photos and graphics
- the pros and cons of moving your business to the cloud
- connecting the dots with the ultimate online office suite
- why you can't afford to ignore the spread of mobile Internet.

THE 'OPEN SOURCE' REVOLUTION

Almost everything you need to know about free software solutions

'Open source' is a term used to describe any piece of computer software for which the 'source code' is available for others to download, improve and adapt. By 'source code' I mean the lines of programming language written to run the software. Think of it as the bricks of a house – the house being the software program itself. You might start by building a bungalow, so you make some bricks and put them together and the house works quite nicely for what you intended. But someone has the idea that an annex containing a pool would improve your house, so they take your bricks and add their own to the mix, releasing a new version of your house with a pool bolted onto the side. The result is a piece of software built for the people, by the people and continually evolving as needs change over time.

Open source 'coders' – the communities who write this software and give it away free online – come from many different backgrounds, and their motivations are varied too. Many are students who have the time and resources to get a little experience, and who perhaps hope to catch the eye of a developer who'll offer them a job when they graduate. They could also be experienced software engineers who want to improve an open source package because they use it themselves. Or they might just be amateur programmers doing it for kudos or as a protest against over-priced commercial software. Whoever they are, they are many and they are very active; there is a buzzing open source software scene offering free alternatives to all the mainstream applications under a liberal 'catch-all' software licence known as 'freeware'.

The other type of free software you'll see a lot is 'shareware'. This is usually a limited version of a full, premium application. The shareware version may have fewer features, or a limited activation period, after which you'll have to upgrade to the paid version if you want to carry on using it. Some are ad supported, with the option to turn off annoying banners if you pay to upgrade.

As the title of this book would suggest, there are also a lot of cloud-based tools that are free to use, and the companies that produce them make their money in a number of different ways. 'Freemium' is a term used to describe services where the core operation is free but you can 'bolt on' useful extras from a kitbag of premium features. Many tools designed to help you manage your contacts and social interactions will keep the really useful analytics hidden behind a premium upgrade, or may limit you on storage or the number of contacts they can process. Many services where users spend a lot of time on their pages, like Facebook for example, also use advertising to generate income.

TIP

Some downloads can contain 'spyware' or 'malware', which is a snip of code that works unseen, usually collecting marketing data or delivering covert advertising. At the most extreme it could be malicious code giving hackers a back door into your system, so make sure that you download stuff only through reputable sites and pay attention to user ratings, as you can bet your life that people will be shouting about it in the download's review section if it contains any nasty malware.

alternativeto.net

Pretty much everything we'll be looking at in this chapter, and a lot more besides, can be found in the AlternativeTo database. At first glance the website is a bit intimidating, with lots of small text blocks littered with important-looking acronyms and technical jargon. This is sadly often the case on a site connected to the open source movement, and it can scare casual surfers away. It's also not that obvious how to browse the contents of the database on this website, as the 'category' bar is tiny. The best way to browse is to choose the platform you're searching for from the bar across the top, such Mac, Windows, tablets or one of the smartphones, and then click one of the microscopic category links in the bar immediately below that. There is a mind-boggling amount of software here, all presented with a short description and links to download pages. There is also a 'likes' button, letting you see which products are most recommended by site users – which could lead you to discover software you didn't even realise you needed.

OPENING WINDOWS

The free alternatives to popular operating systems

When you walk into a shop to buy a computer it usually comes with an operating system installed, like Windows or Mac. This doesn't make the software free, as the cost of the licence is always included (or 'bundled') in the purchase price of the machine. There is no denying that this is the simplest way to set up your computer, as any conflicts with various electronic parts, like graphics cards, motherboards and processor chips, will have already been ironed out for you in the shop. If you're strapped for cash, though, it's worth asking if they will sell you a computer without the software bundled with it. The big retail chains may not offer this, which is understandable really, as there is the potential for a lot of aftercare support in helping you to set up your machine. Most independent computer shops will probably do you a deal, though, meaning that you can opt for one of the many fantastic open source operating systems that have been developed and are supported by a vast community of coding enthusiasts. Aside from the cost implications, commercial software tends to be somewhat bloated, with lots of extra glossy coding and technical baubles designed to catch the consumer's eye. If your old computer or cheap netbook is struggling under the weight of running Windows, a lighter-weight operating system could be the best way to breathe life back into it.

☼ *TIP*

One of the downsides of open source operating systems is that some of the software you use may not be available. Most Linux builds include a link to an 'app store' to browse for free open source applications, so you should be able to find reasonable alternatives for most things.

www.ubuntu.com

Linux is the best known family of open source operating systems and there are dozens of different versions known as 'builds' or 'distributions', and often referred to on discussion boards as 'distros'. Linux is a science in its own right, and I wouldn't presume to call myself anything like an expert. But you don't need to be an expert to find a good working version of the operating system and install it on your machine. Ubuntu is a great version of Linux for beginners to try (and thank you to my army of Linux-crazy Twitter followers for pointing me towards it). Even the name Ubuntu means 'humanity to others' in ancient African, and the project was founded on the principle of bringing quality, free software that anyone can use to the world. The operating system itself is a breeze to use, either out of the 'box', so to speak, or with as much customisation as you have the stomach to apply. Installing it won't be quite such a walk in the park, however. You'll first need to copy the .iso file that you download on the Ubuntu site onto a CD or USB drive, and then configure your computer to look at that CD or USB drive first before starting Windows. It's not simple, but the instructions on the download page are very straightforward to follow – no confusing tech jargon here. If you do have the time and desire to do something completely new you'll be rewarded with a fast, efficient and stable operating system, free and fully supported by an enthusiastic and approachable community of volunteers. You'll also get a lot of respect just for being on Linux, if you choose to hang out in the more geeky forums.

TIP

Installing a new operating system will erase all of the data on that drive, so make sure that you've saved all your personal stuff elsewhere or made a CD/USB drive copy. If your hard drive is partitioned there will be two drive letters listed under 'My Computer'. If the operating system is installed on (C:), your data should be safe if you save it on the other drive. It's definitely advisable to back it up elsewhere too, though, as you can never be too safe when making major system changes.

www.ubuntu.com/download/desktop/windows-installer

So, you're thinking about making the leap to Ubuntu, but what if you don't like it? Once the operating system is installed, the only way to go back is to reinstall your old one, which will require the CDs or other installation files, so make sure that you have them before proceeding. The other option is to use Wubi to make a virtual partition on your hard drive and install a version of Ubuntu on it, just as you would any other program. You don't need to save anything or back it up, and the whole thing is completely reversible by just uninstalling Wubi. Wubi turns your computer into something known as a 'dual-boot system', so when you start it up you have the choice to enter either your Windows or Ubuntu desktop layout. Ubuntu doesn't run anywhere near as fast as the native version when it's installed in the usual way, but this method will definitely let you thoroughly test the software before making a final commitment.

☼ *TIP*

distrowatch.com
Ubuntu may be the easiest way to start you off, but it's by no means the only or even the best Linux option. Linux Mint also comes highly recommended for beginners, while a build called Gnome is said to have a more 'Windows-like experience' for the user. If you want to learn more about the wonderful world of open source systems, DistroWatch provides a complete and very thorough portal to everything that's happening.

THE ESSENTIAL OFFICE

Free software options for every office task

openoffice.org

The next thing on the shopping list is a good, all-round office suite. MS Office is the popular premium option the world over, but you don't need to buy it in order to read and make files that are compatible with everyone else's. OpenOffice is a huge open source project that's been going since the year 2000 and has everything you could want to compete with Microsoft's suite – word processor, spreadsheet, presentation software, drawing package, database and more, all very similar in form and function to their commercial equals, so the learning curve is fairly small (though you may have to hunt for the occasional feature to begin with). It is fully compatible with all mainstream file types and you should be able to open and work on most documents, images and other appropriate files regardless of which application they were created in.

TIP

OpenOffice saves documents as its own file types by default, like .odt for text documents. People using MS Word should still be able to open these files, but you can avoid confusion by using the drop-down menu when you choose ' Save as' and changing the file type to one of the more commonly recognised Microsoft formats.

EMAIL TOOLS AND TIPS

The best cloud solutions for digital communication

Email may have slipped a bit into the shadow of social media lately, but it's still an important marketing tool, and for many mature consumers it remains the preferred way of receiving offers and promotions. The average person receives over 100 emails a day and spends 28 minutes dealing with them. Microsoft Outlook is undeniably the most widely used 'email client' – which is the name given to any piece of software that lets you access your email account for reading, storing, composing and sending replies. Outlook comes bundled in MS Office, with a free, cut-down version in the Windows operating system, so it's really little surprise that it's the market leader. But just because it's there you don't have to use it. You could choose to keep your email in the cloud instead, there are several important benefits, but also an equally important downside. The obvious benefit is that you can access your communication anywhere, from any connected device; the downside is that if you can't get a connection to the Internet you won't be able to read or send any new messages, crippling your work flow. We will look at ways in which you can cut down on the time you spend dealing with email when we meet your virtual assistant in Chapter 7. For now you just need to set yourself up with a preferred method of handling it.

www.mozilla.org/thunderbird

One of the most popular desktop alternatives to Microsoft's email offering is Thunderbird, made by the same people who make the Firefox browser that you may be familiar with. The download is free and your messages are stored on your computer, where you can set up several different email accounts to monitor through one window. It's a great email client, giving you all the control you need with no fuss and, most importantly, with tight security in place. Spam or junk email is dealt with automatically too, so you can just concentrate on genuine messages.

mail.google.com

If you have enough faith in the cloud and your ability to connect to it without interruption, Gmail is a very popular choice, with the huge benefit of being a well-crafted fit when it comes to integrating with Google's many other business products. We've already spoken about a couple of neat social plug-ins that you can use with Gmail, but that barely scratches the surface of what is out there if you really want to supercharge your email. You access folders through a browser, or there are fancier ways to connect if you want to investigate third-party applications. There are also apps for mobile and tablet computers, making it easy to link up popular online email accounts so that you can access them on the move – some apps are even beginning to offer 'offline browsing' modes, which let you download a chunk of content to your local memory when on WiFi so that you're not completely stuck if your connection goes down.

outlook.com

If you're leaning more towards the Microsoft route but want to keep emails in the cloud, you can try Outlook as an online email service instead. Like Gmail, you access everything through the browser. This is Microsoft's rebranding of its long-time popular email service Hotmail, so it is well supported by mobile and third-party applications as well.

essentialpim.com

Despite all the fancy features offered by the mainstream email clients, sometimes you just want a quick and convenient way to get at your stuff, whatever situation you find yourself in. EssentialPIM (personal information manager) lets you manage your contacts, email and calendar through an interface that looks very much like Outlook. There is a free trial of the full service that lets you link up multiple accounts and sync them across all desktop and mobile devices. You can even install the application on a USB drive that you put in your pocket and take with you. When you need to access your email or calendar just plug the USB stick into any computer you can get your hands on and the software will fire up, even if it's not connected to the Internet. The most useful features, sadly, go away after the trial, after which you'll have to pay $40 to keep the pro version.

TIP

If your business is a private or public limited company or a Limited Liability Partnership, the Companies Act 1985 requires all of your business emails to include:

- *your company's registered name (e.g. XYZ Ltd)*
- *your company registration number*
- *your place of registration (e.g. Scotland or England & Wales)*
- *your registered office address.*

TIP

unroll.me
Over time you may have signed up for lots of services that send you junk mail, such as website registrations, newsletters and groups. Unroll.me is a handy Gmail plug-in that spots subscription emails and stores them safely out of sight, sending you a short summary of what you've received if you want. The plug-in doesn't actually unsubscribe you from the services but saves the emails in another folder. You can reverse the process at any time to keep seeing the emails arrive in your inbox.

www.gotfreefax.com

Hardly anyone uses fax any more, but you may occasionally need to send one, especially if you're ordering goods or resources from far-flung countries. You don't need to fork out any cash on office equipment if you just want to send the occasional fax message. GotFreeFax.com is one of a few similar services that let you load up a document from your computer and send it as a fax. The service is free, but ad supported both on the website and with the insertion of an advert into the cover page of your message; double whammy — you and your recipient both see the advertisement, so you're kind of paying for the fax service in a roundabout way.

Profile

Tony Banks, Founder of Balhousie Care Group

"I like my fellow man and I think humility is one of the biggest qualities that any leader can have, although it's a quality that's not talked about enough in business circles."

Tony Banks is a leading Scottish entrepreneur and founder of Balhousie Care Group, a venture that he started after seeing an opportunity to create a family business at a time when Margaret Thatcher was encouraging more regulation in the care home industry, moving it away from unregulated bed-and-breakfast accommodation and long-stay hospitals to environments that provided a much higher standard of care. An ex-army man, he is also the author of acclaimed war biography *Storming the Falklands: My War and After*, published in March 2012. He shot to media fame in 2009 when he took part in Channel 4's *The Secret Millionaire*, living anonymously on a poverty-stricken estate in Anfield. He was so moved by the experience that he ended up donating hundreds of thousands of pounds to the people whom he met while filming. He believes it is an experience that changed his life completely: inspired by the fighting spirit of the most disadvantaged people in life, he was helped to refocus his energy on things like family and relationships. Tony also serves on the boards of the Scottish Entrepreneurial Exchange and the Enemy Within Appeal for Combat Stress.

Tony said:
I've worked pretty much from the age of 11 – delivering milk or newspapers, emptying bins and making badges to sell at school – because I came from a working-class background where money was tight, so knew I was going to have to do things for myself if I wanted those little 'extras' in life. I learnt important lessons about being an entrepreneur from my time in the army; even

though it's a very disciplined and structured environment, it's also very freethinking and task-orientated in the military. You know you have to get the job done with the resources that you have available, and in a combat situation those resources could be depleted really quickly because guys are getting killed around you; but you still have to get the job done. I think it also gave me the ability to work long and unusual hours and to go that extra mile, which is very important when you're starting a business. Taking part in *Secret Millionaire* was absolutely a life-changing experience. To see the tremendous spirit that disadvantaged people have and their fight to overcome adversity made me rethink and refocus my priorities. It was a very humbling experience. I like my fellow man and I think humility is one of the biggest qualities that any leader can have, although it's a quality that's not talked about enough in business circles. Since the recession hit in 2008 I have never known the economic conditions to be so tough, and even though analysts are talking about a recovery in 2014, personally I don't see it myself at the moment. It's really important that people deal with the stress of running a business by talking about it with others who have been through the same experiences. I do a lot of work with the charity Combat Stress and have learnt that it can take a few years for the effects to manifest. Being an entrepreneur is a very lonely existence because the buck stops with you and nobody says 'Well done, what a great job you've done.' You've got to learn to praise yourself and share the burden of your issues with your networks or mentors, or if you can afford it, get professional coaching because that will really help you cope as a new start-up business. The Internet makes networks and information more freely available and it is 100% essential for new businesses to embrace this technology. When I started my care home business 20 years ago the families who were placing their loved ones with us were not computer savvy, but in the last five years that has completely changed. Now everyone starts their research online because all the information they need is there and they don't have to spend time in the car visiting lots of different places.

They can also see if any negative comments have been made, so it is hugely important that you have a good website, updated regularly with all the right information, and that people can find you when they do an Internet search.

PICTURE PERFECT

Tools for editing photos and graphics

If you want to work seriously with pictures, like making flyers or posters or editing photographic work, you're going to need something with a little more oomph than the free 'Paint' tool that comes with Windows. There are many choices in this field, with some really unusual styles and filters available that make creating a work of art really easy, even for complete beginners. You'll have to explore on your own if you want to get really creative, as that is too far off-topic for this particular tome (it's one of the topics high on my list of possibilities for the next book, though!). A good search term to investigate if you're interested in learning more is 'free image effects editor' – which you'll find in abundance online. The benefit of using an online service is that your images are stored on the Internet, so you can access and work on them from any connected computer. Like every other cloud service we've looked at, there are pros and cons to relying on a net connection to get any work done – plus you'll have to spend some time uploading your images to the service from your computer, which could take a while if they are very high resolution and you're connection isn't that fast.

getgimp.com

If you're already using Adobe's Photoshop you don't need to pay £500 for the premium package to work in the same way at home. GIMP is an excellent open source download that is so like its commercial counterpart that you will hardly notice the switchover. The website even proudly displays the tagline "Like Photoshop only 100% free", and because it is open source there are a lot of enthusiasts making extra bells and whistles to customise and tweak the program's performance. These extras are little packets of software known as plug-ins or add-ons, which, upon installation, make some minor change to the interface or operation of an application. In the case of GIMP this might be a filter to add a special effect, or increasing the number of file types that are supported. Going back to our building analogy, a plug-in might be a small sack of bricks that individuals can use to add a nice custom barbecue in the garden of their bungalow.

TIP

If you think back to Chapter 1, we spoke about protecting images posted online with a watermark. Use the 'layers' feature in GIMP to add a copyright message in a size and style that suits you, and then just reduce the percentage of opacity for that layer to a transparency that doesn't interfere too much with the image that you want to show off.

fotoflexer.com

If you want to stick with the cloud when editing your snaps, FotoFlexer has a fully featured image editor with some really nice filters and advanced effects that are perfect for working with photographs – including a blemish and wrinkle fixer for those times when you weren't looking your best. All the standard tools you'd expect from a desktop image editor are included, plus some fancy extras under the 'geek' tab (though you will probably need to follow the tutorials to operate them, as they are fairly advanced). You don't even need to register – just upload an image or grab one from the web or one of the many social sharing sites that are supported. Once it's finished, save your image on your local hard drive or post it straight to your preferred sharing site, ready for embedding into your website or blog. If you do register with the site you can save stuff in the cloud to work on from another device.

inkscape.org

Inkscape is the open source alternative to Adobe's Illustrator application, which, if you work in design, you will recognise as being the industry-standard vector graphics editor. If that means nothing to you, needless to say you can walk on by here without worrying. But if you are a struggling graphic designer trying to set up shop on your own you can save up to £400 by not shelling out for Adobe's vector graphics editor, as this one works every bit as well as the commercial package.

PROUD TO GO CLOUD

The pros and cons of moving your business to the cloud completely

To cloud or not to cloud? That is the real question these days. It's the subject of lively, ongoing debate; and with technology growing and morphing so rapidly in this field, the only certainty is that you do need to be online, somehow. But whether upping sticks and moving to the cloud from an established office-based set-up is best for *your* business depends on a lot of factors. Doing so will no doubt slash overheads, especially if you're getting rid of an office building to work collaboratively in an online team space – although you need to be very sure that you trust your team before making such a big change. Some people find it hard to motivate themselves when working from home, so you'd be smart to start from a position of regular and transparent task sharing and progress reports right from the outset. You're better off being a little heavy handed to begin with and you can loosen the reins a little once everyone has settled into a new pattern of working.

For those starting a business from scratch, the attraction of working in the cloud is hard to deny. You can be up and running in no time, with minimal costs and able to move and change direction at the drop of a hat without incurring extra overheads. It's well documented that around half of all start-ups fail in the first year, so keeping your outlay down by having a virtual office will take away some of the cash-flow pressure – plus you'll have fewer physical assets to offload if it does all go pear-shaped in the end.

So, financially it makes a lot of sense for certain types of business to work in the cloud, but operationally there are huge benefits too. All of your data, be that email, calendar, quotes, correspondence, legal documents, images, plans, whatever, is just there for you any time you want to fire up an Internet browser or third-party app to work with it. No one will touch your files or move stuff around while you're out (unless you are working collaboratively in a team, and even then there will be a record of what they have done) and you won't forget to take any files, such as a vital presentation, with you on a USB stick. As I've already alluded, though, having everything stored in the cloud could end up being pretty crippling if you can't get online, and this is one of the main arguments bandied about by cloud critics. On the flip side, you might experience a catastrophic event at home or in the office – imagine suffering a fire or flood that killed not only your Internet connection but a lot of your equipment too. With all your work and applications stored in the cloud, you could pitch up at any other location and continue working straight away, with minimum downtime for your business. Working in the cloud, you have an in-built 'complete disaster recovery plan', as your data is stored off-site and so there is no chance of it being lost in a local disaster – although, if you're following one of the backup plans we spoke of in Chapter 4, this shouldn't really be an issue.

 TIP

tos-dr.info
How many times have you clicked 'agree' to the terms and conditions without actually reading them? It's been called the "biggest lie on the web", but Terms of Service: Didn't Read is building a database for people who actually HAVE read the terms to highlight the important bits and give all the mainstream web services an easy-to-understand rating.

Ultimately, security has to be a big concern and you'll find plenty of opinion both for and against the cloud if you care to research it. Before making any major commitment with your valuable private data you should check the service's credentials (all good cloud service providers should have encryption and security details clearly displayed on their website) and read plenty of reviews on well-respected websites to ensure that you're choosing the best service available at the time. Most mainstream providers like the ones mentioned in this book will have pretty high-level defences in place and there are often add-ons available if you want to take more precautions. But it's fair to say that nothing in this world is indestructible – although statistically speaking you are unlikely to find yourself the focus of a targeted 'hacking' attempt. I would imagine that most readers will end up taking a combination of both routes at first, perhaps keeping certain private aspects of their business on the desktop while they start building trust in cloud suppliers with the more trivial office tasks.

TIP

'Hacking' is a term used in the popular press to describe 'breaking into' a computer system by circumventing its security, often with the goal of stealing or corrupting the information it contains. More broadly, the term can apply to non-malicious activities too, like adapting and customising retail electronics and computer equipment or making innovative changes to open source software programs.

CLOUD CENTRAL

Bringing your complete online office together under one roof

www.google.com/apps/business

If you decide to take that leap and work completely in the cloud, we've already looked at many options for storing, working with and sharing documents and content online. If you're beginning to think about a unified solution, with an ever-growing box of business resources the undisputed king of the all-in-one solution has to be Google. We explored Dashboard, where you can link up all those online activities into one centrally controlled hub, at the end of Chapter 1. If you're going the Google cloud route it's worth signing up for an 'Apps for Business' account. The free service bundles Gmail, Calendar, Docs and Team Sites (which help you to manage team projects) for a maximum of 10 people working in the cloud and 10GB of storage, and, according to the latest press release, this basic service will be free through to the end of 2013. As ever, there are upgrades for more people and storage, plus some other deeper business tools if you really take to the platform. You'll need to set aside about 30 minutes to get it up and running, and if you're using your own personal domain name (for example WorkingTheCloud.biz) and have already set up your Gmail account and verified your domain name for Google Analytics (as discussed in Chapter 3) this will be a lot quicker and very painless. If you haven't got round to buying your own personalised URL yet, there's the option to set up your Google Apps account with the purchase of a web address seamlessly included, with current prices stated as starting from $8 a year. It may not be the cheapest way of buying that URL, but for a negligible amount it will certainly be the way that gives you the least number of headaches at this stage of the game. There are video tutorials for every step of the way that are easy enough to follow. As well as having lots of programs and apps that you can add to your team dashboard, this system will provide all your staff with a professional-looking, unified email address, using the domain name that you verified, when they sign up to join your team (in my case, that would be kate@WorkingTheCloud.biz) without you having to run an email client serving lots of people through your website. This is very handy, as I can imagine that a lot of you would have no idea how to even start setting that up; and you can just add more people as you take on staff. When staff are collaborating on documents the live chat and real-time changes features are also very handy, as team members can have the same files open at once and be sure that they are all working on the identical and most recent copy. Plus, the dashboard will tell you who logged on when and what they accessed, which provides a very good way of keeping an eye on staff productivity without being too intrusive.

GOING MOBILE

Why you can't afford to ignore the spread of mobile Internet

One of the most appealing aspects of moving your business to the cloud has to be the freedom of mobile access. Time is the most precious commodity for any new start-up, and if you can spend idle moments on the train updating your project sheet or answering emails you'll find keeping on top of your administration much easier. Believe it or not, more people currently own a mobile phone (5.1 billion) than own a toothbrush (4.2 billion), and, as I mentioned before, the number of Internet-connected devices around the world looks set to continue growing at a phenomenal rate. Tablet computers are booming; just two years after launch, Apple had shipped 67 million iPads; it took the company 24 years to sell that many desktop Macs. About 40% of new handsets (1.2 billion) entering the market over the next five years will be smartphones of every flavour and the number of corporations buying into the tech will grow by 50% year on year. It's hard to ignore numbers like this and there are a lot of players entering the mobile apps market right now. The other benefit (or curse, depending on your viewpoint) this market has is a relatively low barrier to entry. These days, you can make apps for sale using free software, and a lot of people are – though there are also lots of first-class professional outfits coming up as well. This means that there is lots of innovation, and pretty well all of the mainstream websites and tools I've mentioned in this book have some kind of smartphone or tablet app to download. They may be paid apps, being one of the added 'extra features' that help a free service provider to turn a profit, but you'll find that a lot of them cost nothing to download and use. It's worth checking if your mobile platform is supported when you sign up with a service, as it could radically improve your productivity.

It's also worth remembering that a growing number of your customers and clients are likely to be using smartphones. In the first quarter of 2012 there were an astounding 100 billion mobile Internet sessions logged worldwide, with users spending as much time on social media apps (24 minutes a day on average) as they spent playing mobile games. Nearly half of mobile surfers like to share video and audio via Facebook, so take this into consideration when making content to share. Will it look good on a mobile screen too? If not, maybe simplify your design a bit.

Again, I need to give a very serious nod to security here, but I'm not going to bang on and on about it – use your favourite search engine for that. It is very important that you know what you're downloading, though, and how much information you're giving away to the developer – or worse, to the Internet at large. For example, if you agree to let an app use 'location services' and then use it to post photos from your living room, that map location will be viewable by anyone who can access the photograph, to within just a few dozen yards of your front door. You should also know that not all apps are made equal – and some can seriously impair the performance of your smartphone, draining the battery lightning-fast or even introducing malicious code if they're not from a reputable source. Apple's devices are a little more protected, as the company has a strict approval process before an app can appear in the store. Android is the 'open source' mobile option, so you'll find a lot more free and random stuff listed, but the download market doesn't have the same approval layers as Apple, so you need to be very sure about what you're downloading.

TIP

If you find an app that you want to try out and it's not from a mainstream source, run a quick Internet search first to see what other people are saying about it.

Anyone's mobile could become the target of hackers, as the high-profile 'phone hacking' scandal that began in 2005 illustrates, but sticking with respected mainstream services for sensitive and business applications should be ample protection for most. You might also lose your phone, so you'd better have it password-locked when not in use, or (not to put too fine a point on it) you are a fool; and a fool and his data are soon parted. There are plenty of apps that can give you added protection if you search the app market for your particular device, and we'll be looking at some of them in Chapter 8.

TIP

Be aware of who might be looking over your shoulder. On tablet devices especially it is easy to see when a person types a password to access the device or to log in to an online account. Obviously, never do your banking in a public place and make sure that no one is sneaking a look over your shoulder when you are typing sensitive data.

www.lookout.com

Lookout Mobile Security is a great peace-of-mind app for most mobile formats. Just enter your number on the website and it will link up to your handset, backing up all your contacts and pictures so that you can access them through the browser. With the app running, your phone will be constantly scanned and updated to guard against the latest security threats. Your activity will be monitored and a warning will pop up on screen if you're doing anything risky, like connecting to an unsecured WiFi network or downloading a malicious app. When you do install a new app, Lookout will flag up any potential security risks in the permissions you're being asked to agree to, so that you can make a more informed choice (without having to read the small print yourself, I want to point out!). If you do lose your phone, the website will show you where it is using GPS, even asking it to scream, which is useful if it's slipped down the back of the sofa. In a worst-case scenario, you can remotely lock or even wipe the contents of your mobile, so that at least your private information won't get into the hands of the criminals along with your phone. The service is free, with some extras if you want to go premium. As well as the security features, Lookout performs a regular backup of all your contacts, photos and other data on your phone.

 TIP

Upgrading your phone can be stressful when it comes to transferring all your contacts and content from one handset to another. Use Lookout to back up all your data and then just restore it to the new phone. Job done.

CASH FLOW HEAVEN

Having cleared your bottom line of any unnecessary cash drains, you should now have a pretty *sweet* office *suite* up and running on your computer at a fraction of the cost you'd expect. Why waste money on commercial applications when you can achieve the exact same results free of charge? Right? I can't believe that more people don't think this way. And free doesn't have to mean cheap or without any value. You can work to completely professional standards using the downloads and online applications featured in this chapter, and you'll find the open source communities who choose to support them only too happy to help if you run into problems or discover a bug, or even have a suggestion to improve the application. Cloud-based solutions that let you 'rent' software when you need it, rather than buying a full licence up front, should also save you cash, especially if you're engaging remote workers and casual staff and want them all working on a unified platform. In the old days you'd have had to pay a full licence for each of them – now you effectively just push 50 pence pieces in the app-meter and people clock in when they need to. It's not stingy, it's financially smart – something we're going to be talking about a lot more in the next chapter as we go prospecting for the many money-saving secrets that are to be unearthed online.

Chapter 6

The money cloud

Cost-cutting and money management tools

So far we've looked at lots of ways in which you can cut the cost of setting up and running your business by harnessing the power of the cloud. But there are many more practical, money-saving tactics that you can employ both on and offline. There's the obvious stuff like setting your printer to draft mode and switching off lights and equipment at the end of the day. Did you know that leaving your printer in standby mode is the same as burning a 40-watt light bulb overnight? Or you could choose to make your accounts system fully digital, saving time, faff and money by emailing invoices and statements instead of posting them. When it comes to tracking your money, a digital paper trail is a lot easier to follow than the old-fashioned type, too. Online invoicing tools will tell you exactly when your invoice has been viewed, so there can be no more convenient 'denial of receipt' when it comes to settling an account. You could even save a ton of cash by exchanging heavy, paper catalogues for digital ones. With the image-editing tools we've already looked at you can make a very attractive showcase for your products, with links to click directly through to point of purchase. No printing costs; no postage costs; no waiting time for customers to receive them. Personally, I object to receiving paper catalogues through my letterbox anyway, as it's a needless waste of natural resources and I would much rather browse a company's products online. This chapter concentrates on protecting your bottom line by keeping the outgoings to a minimum without negatively impacting on your productivity. The key areas we will cover in the following pages are:

- finding the right workspace for your business
- setting up a home office
- interview with Martin Lewis, the Money Saving Expert
- group buying for the best deals
- free phone calls and instant messenger services
- reviving the ancient tradition of barter in a high-tech trade environment
- financial tools and accounting services.

THINKING OUT OF THE BOX

Letting go of your physical workspace

Depending on the size and nature of your business, you could think about getting rid of a physical office altogether, saving on rent, insurance, utility bills and even stationery supplies. You could work at home or move into a shared office space, such as an enterprise hub or serviced communal building. This can be a great way to mix with your peers and keep socially active in your working environment if you don't think you'll flourish being alone. If you do decide to fly completely solo, a home office could also reduce your taxes, as you'll be able to offset a certain percentage of your mortgage/rent and running costs to cover the overheads of your business. There are plenty of great places online where you can find out the right information for you, so make sure that you do your homework before filling out your tax return. If you're really running on a shoestring you could even flit from coffee shop to coffee shop, taking micro-sips of your latte while abusing their free WiFi connection and power supply — an increasingly popular practice that's become known as 'cappuccino commerce'. As long as the venue isn't too crowded and you actually buy something from time to time no one will bat an eyelid. This trend is really booming in the UK right now, with a recent study showing that around 22% of companies started in the last three years base themselves in bars and coffee shops to keep overheads down. It's worth remembering, though, that the WiFi connection may not be secure and accessing the Internet can get quite slow when the network is being used heavily by other customers.

www.worksnug.com

If you don't mind a fairly transient lifestyle but don't want to spend your days in a coffee shop, WorkSnug offers a fine solution to searching for a temporary place to rest your weary laptop. The database is overflowing with mobile worker-friendly environments, both free and public (so all those coffee shops are listed here too), but it also lists more formal office set-ups and pay-as-you-go hot-desking spaces if you want something a little more business-like. You can search for an office through the website or, if you have an Android, iPhone, BlackBerry or Nokia OVI smartphone, download the free app and use the location feature to find a suitable space nearby. Details about what services each location offers are displayed, such as power and free Internet connections; and because noise is important in any communal workspace it even tells you how loud the space is generally, based on the experience of site members who've been there before you. You can also add a workspace if you come across a good location that isn't already listed.

twitraffic.co.uk

If you do have to travel to the office by car you can save time and money by keeping ahead of the traffic with Twitraffic. This app for Android and iPhone is fuelled by tweeters mentioning certain watchwords picked up by the service and linked to a location: words like traffic, accident, fire, slow, congestion, junction, road works and queues. Apparently we like to tweet about bad traffic, as the app processes four live tweets per second covering the UK alone. The speed at which Twitter spreads information is a powerful feature for a service like this, making it your best chance for finding out about changing conditions as they actually unfold. According to the website's creators, "Twitraffic reports incidents, on average, 7.1 minutes before the UK government's Highways Agency data". The app is currently free on Android but will set you back 69p on iPhone. It only covers the UK and USA right now, with plans to expand into South Africa in the months ahead.

GOING POSTAL CODE

Creating the right environment to do business from your home

There can be nothing more liberating than beginning your first day's work with a 10-second commute to the office. If you're self-motivated enough to work at home (which not everyone is) you'll enjoy no more traffic jams, no overcrowded public transport or being soaked by a thoughtless driver speeding through a puddle right beside you. You won't have to pay £2.50 for coffee in a cardboard cup, and domestic chores will become less of an intrusion in your life as you can put the laundry on a dozen times throughout the day with no real impact on your productivity. If you set aside dedicated space and equipment in your home that will be used only for business you can even save money on tax, offsetting a portion of everything you pay to run your home against your tax bill. I'm not a tax expert, and personally I choose to pay an accountant to finalise my tax return because I've never been terribly confident with numbers, but it's entirely possible to do everything yourself online if you want to – and, contrary to the pained expression on my face when I wrote that line, you don't have to be a mathematical genius either. The only website you'll need for information on UK tax is www.hmrc.gov.uk, where there are simple guides and submission forms designed to make it as easy as possible for you to pay your tax – it is in the government's interest to get your cash into the coffers, after all.

 TIP

If you're having trouble understanding tax law, why not use the Get Lunched networking website covered in Chapter 2 to take a friendly accountant you know from LinkedIn out for lunch? This could be an inexpensive (and enjoyable) way to get enough professional advice for you to know what your next steps should be.

So, you've decided to take the plunge and set up a formal office at home. Make an event of it, maybe setting a 'date to move in' and marking the occasion in the same way that you might celebrate starting a new job – it will give you a target to shoot for and help to build the excitement for both you and those people who are supporting you. Whatever happens, you're probably going to need to rearrange some of your furniture, as you'll be far more productive if you have a dedicated (and ideally isolated) space to work in.

TIP

It's all very well turning the spare bedroom into an office, but if your kids are crawling around under the desk and you have neighbours popping in every five minutes for coffee you might as well go back to the sofa and chill out; you're not going to be doing much work anyway. Make sure that anyone who lives with you or is likely to visit knows the rules about business and personal space.

www.floorplanner.com

Before you start pulling your home apart to set up your brand new office you can save time by thoroughly planning the eventual layout with the free interior design tool from Floorplanner. The drag-and-drop interface is simplicity itself, a real joy to use. Setting up your floor plan initially takes a little time to get right, but once you have it saved you can start playing around with the layout of your furniture to your heart's content; and there's an impressive range of fixtures and fittings available. The basic account is free for personal use and lets you save one design. It would be far too simplistic for professional designers but if you just want to tinker around as an amateur you can't really go wrong. Switch to 3D mode to get a sense of how your arrangement will feel in reality.

TIP

Floorplanner gives you an embed code and links for sharing your design with other people. If you're changing the layout of your shop or cafe, asking your customers for input could be a really nice way to engage them in the refurbishment and generate interest in the end results – plus, they might even have some brilliant ideas.

Profile

Martin Lewis, Money Saving Expert

"I wish I had been clever enough to invent Money Saving Expert the way it is, but it grew organically; if I had expected such success I would have probably got it terribly wrong."

Martin Lewis is the 'Money Saving Expert' – consumer finance guru, TV and radio presenter, newspaper columnist and best-selling author – and the man behind the UK's number one money site, MoneySavingExpert.com, which gets around 14 million unique visitors a month. A trained personal finance and business journalist who studied at the London School of Economics, Martin first became the Money Saving Expert when he worked for a small TV channel called 'Simply Money', where he suggested a show that used hard-core analytical research to uncover the best consumer finance deals each day. Like the TV show, the website appeals to the bargain hunter in us by revealing straightforward ways for consumers to cut down on their bills and living expenses without having to sacrifice quality of life. It has also been the driving force behind several high-profile campaigns to get a fairer deal for consumers in areas such as bank charges, PPI payments and, in the latest campaign, reclaiming care home fees. Martin set up the site in 2003, working out of his back bedroom, at a cost of £100. Less than a decade later the brand was sold for a cool £87 million – although far from this being a lucrative exit strategy, Martin remains in tight control of the editorial, as he was keen to explain when we spoke.

Martin said:
I wish I had been clever enough to invent Money Saving Expert the way it is, but it grew organically; if I had expected such success I would have probably got it terribly wrong. When I set

it up it had no way of making money and I only introduced that in a very ethical way once it got too much for me, as a jobbing journalist, to be able to afford the £1,000 a month it was starting to cost to run the website. As it's grown I've always employed the mantra 'never spend more money than I've got', so I took on more staff to expand only as the money came in. Of course, for the last four or five years I've known it become big and huge and valuable, but for me the sale to MoneySupermarket was far more about giving the website a future no matter what happens to me, so I had a couple of unusual clauses worked into the deal. First, we have agreed an editorial code which says the parent company has no control over editorial and the site must be run in the best interests of the consumer and not for its owner's own financial purposes. The other is that my 'earn-out' (which is the part of the deal that says over three years I can earn more than the original pay-out for the sale) is based on the website growing its audience and maintaining trust rather than any financial metrics. It is the most trusted site of its kind at the moment and I will be rewarded if it continues to remain so in the years ahead. So for the users this sale will not change a thing—we will be putting up the same kind of content as we've always put up and running the same kinds of campaigns; and I have absolute control over the editorial. Twenty years ago it wouldn't have been possible for one journalist to set up a publication in his back bedroom that within 10 years competes with the national newspapers. Only the Internet allows that to happen because of its mass reach, but there are many challenges as well. I always say it's very easy to set up a successful website; all you need is unique content that nobody else has got and then to tell millions of people about it. As long as you can do those two things, it won't be a problem.

TIP

According to a study by consumer watchdog Which?, Tuesdays are the cheapest day of the week to fly out of the UK.

www.moneysavingexpert.com

MoneySavingExpert.com is the UK's leading website for advice on money matters, taking a 'daily deals' approach to sniffing out the best (and often hidden) options for every aspect of consumer and household spending. Whether it's getting the best prices for energy, insurance, bank charges and interest rates, or taking advantage of the many discounts and vouchers uncovered by the site's independent researchers, Martin's philosophy for the website is not about being 'tight' but rather about getting value for money, knowing your rights and making sure you don't pay a penny more than you need in order to live life exactly the way you want. Almost 8 million subscribers receive the free weekly email digest and visitors are encouraged to use the 'Money Makeover' guide to see if they can achieve "the equivalent of a 25% pay rise by being an active, savvy consumer and shifting to the very best deals". As well as copious insightful articles and important national campaigns, there is an active and supportive forum community where users share experiences and encourage each other to become debt free, despite often arriving at the community in a desperate financial situation.

TIP

www.hoteltonight.com
If you need a last-minute hotel because a meeting overran, treat yourself to something better than a budget flop-house with the Hotel Tonight smartphone app. The service negotiates daily with a handful of hotels in three budget categories to bring you deals up to 70% cheaper than list price. There are some really lovely hotel rooms going for a song in major cities across the world.

splitticket.moneysavingexpert.com

One of the side projects recently launched by MoneySavingExpert.com is TicketySplit, a web-based and smartphone app that looks at cross-country UK train journeys and uncovers the cheapest possible way to buy your tickets. It saves you cash by splitting the journey up and revealing the cheapest ticket for each leg rather than just ordering a complete round trip. Why it is less expensive to plan your journey like this remains a mysterious quirk of the UK rail system. In the app's own words it is "simply because train fares and logic go together like Coco Pops and ketchup".

 TIP

www.transferwithme.com
If you're travelling abroad, save money by getting to and from the airport with other travellers using TransferWithMe.com. This simple networking service lets you hook up with those catching the same flight so you can all save cash sharing the transfer cost or taxi fare.

BUYING BY NUMBERS

Maximise purchasing power through group buying

Another phenomenon that is continuing to spread rapidly through the Internet is 'crowd buying', where discount offers are made for a limited period and will be honoured only if enough people sign up. It takes the risk out of running a great promotion, as you won't take a single penny from your customers until you have enough orders to make the knockdown price profitable. Websites that offer these deals to consumers (such as Groupon, LivingSocial and Wowcher, to name but a few) are known as 'daily deals' or 'voucher' services. From a standing start a few years back, the market has exploded: in the second half of 2011 UK shoppers spent almost £300 million on daily deals websites, buying everything from loft ladders to leg waxing, with an average saving of 56%. There are literally thousands of different websites like this based in Europe alone. The global market was worth almost $900 million in 2010 and forecast to reach $4 billion by 2014. The rise of these websites can be a real benefit to small businesses, as it puts them on a level playing field with the biggest corporations when it comes to marketing promotions, plus when you offer a deal it's included in the voucher company's regular digest, which is usually delivered to registered members by email. People sign up to daily deals websites expecting to receive email notifications, so if you have a consumer product or service to promote it can be a really effective way of getting in front of potential consumers without annoying people by sending unsolicited spam email. Even if you don't make enough sales to fulfil the deal, anyone who *did* sign up is now aware of your business, and it's possible some may even come and buy from you directly anyway. Which voucher company is right for you will depend on a lot of factors, like audience reach and how much it charges, and you'll have to research this for yourself.

www.huddlebuy.co.uk

Voucher companies are normally aimed at the consumer market, but there is one variation on the theme that should interest readers of this book. Huddlebuy is the largest B2B daily deals site in Europe and, as such, has offers that should interest entrepreneurs, start-ups and small businesses. Whether that's training, accounting services, marketing help, office supplies and technical equipment or a professionally built website, Huddlebuy puts group-buying discounts to equal a much larger company's purchasing power into the hands of the sole trader and home worker. Even if you don't see a deal to entice you, it's well worth browsing around sites like this to read articles and features that have been written to encourage that entrepreneurial spirit that will nurture good customers of the service.

www.friendfund.com

Create your own group deals by connecting with other small business owners in your networks who need similar supplies as you do, and together negotiate a discount for volume. You can take some of the risk out of financing this kind of agreement by using a service like friendfund, which lets you set up a collection for whatever it is you're buying and, just like the voucher websites, no money will be taken from anyone's credit cards or PayPal accounts until everyone has paid up within the 10-day deadline. The pool is free to set up and promote through all the popular social hang-outs, and the final amount can be redeemed in

Amazon vouchers or through a PayPal account for a 3% surcharge, so be sure to build that cost into the total purchase price, and confirm that your supplier accepts payment by PayPal.

 TIP

www.ebooboos.com
To find amazing deals on eBay, visit EBooBoos, a simple site designed to spot auction typos. Click the country flag to search your local eBay. What is listed is going to be a complete lottery, so don't go looking for anything specific. Designer labels are a good example of the kinds of high-value items that can go for an absolute song just because no one will see them in the listings.

 TIP

Never be afraid to ask for a discount or wholesale price, even if there are no offers being advertised. Many independent suppliers look at the long-term picture as the economy rides out this financial storm and will support the small business owners who are likely to be their growth customers in the future with special prices. It never hurts to ask, but always ask with confidence.

IP PHONE HOME

Eliminate the cost of making phone calls

The telephone is probably one of the most important pieces of technology that you have in your office, but when it comes to a landline connection you may be surprised to learn that it runs on an infrastructure that hasn't changed in almost a century. In theory, you could plumb a 1920s antique telephone into your wall jack and make a call on it just fine. Since those early days when telephone companies had to physically lay the cable to connect point A to point B we've been used to paying for the service, 'renting' the wire between callers for however many minutes, or even seconds, we are using it. But the Internet has spawned another disruptive technology that is completely changing the face of the telecoms sector. Voice over Internet Protocol (commonly referred to as VoIP) is the technology used to carry a 'voice' over the Internet, allowing VoIP service providers to offer free person-to-person voice, and now video, connections using the infrastructure of the Internet rather than the telecoms networks. VoIP is actually a well-established technology; market leader Skype first launched an early service in 2003, but increasing broadband penetration and the mass adoption of Internet-connected mobile phones across the globe has seen a recent explosion in the number of VoIP users. Now most people you might want to speak to on the phone have an Internet connection, many of them carrying it around in their pocket; so why exactly would you pay by the minute to speak to them when you can speak free of charge online?

Despite this market being a slow starter, 22% of European households with an Internet connection now use VoIP, and according to a recent survey the majority of UK CIOs (Chief Information Officers) believe that the landline will be redundant within five years (I have lived in my current home for seven years and have never once plugged in a landline phone). That's not to say that the landline will die off completely, as there will always be someone standing behind the technology curve and we don't want to leave them high and dry; modern VoIP services get round this with the ability to 'call out' for the cost of a local call – meaning that they transport your connection as far as it can go over the Internet before jumping off onto the telecoms network to complete the last leg of the journey. This is great for international calls, as you can drastically cut down on your phone bills by being charged for only a local call. Better still, persuade your customer or client to sign up to a service like Skype so that you can speak to them free of charge. As well as the cost-saving aspects of VoIP, it delivers compelling enhancements over traditional phone calling, as you'll see in the coming paragraphs.

www.skype.com
For anyone just starting out with VoIP, the obvious choice is market leader Skype. For starters, lots of people have accounts – 250 million

users at present, and 40% year-on-year growth is predicted – so your contacts are likely to be on board already. Once you've signed up and downloaded the software you can add contacts, and will be able to see when they are online and available to talk. Likewise, you can flag your account as busy or available, depending on your situation. Once you're in a call with someone it's easy to invite other users to join you in a conference call. You can also send and receive text messages and attachments such as photographs and documents while you're chatting; and if you have a webcam attached to your computer there is the option to make a video call. If the person you want to speak to doesn't have access to the Internet you'll need to put some credit in your account with Skype; you can then dial their number in exactly the same way that you would for a standard telephone call and Skype will route you as far as possible free of charge, before transferring your call at a local rate to the number you're contacting.

 TIP

If you can't get used to the idea of speaking to people through your computer, Skype sells a handset starting at a little over £50 that connects you to all of the cash-saving benefits of VoIP on your broadband connection through the traditional-feeling medium of a cordless telephone handset.

shop.skype.com/apps

Like other established brands and technologies we've already spoken about, Skype has been around long enough to have built up an impressive arsenal of third-party apps and add-ons, many of which are free to download through the Skype app store. Here you'll find things like real-time language translators so that you can talk to your customers in foreign places and an interactive whiteboard for sharing ideas visually in an online meeting. There are also any number of note-taking, call-recording and sharing tools, some even linked to other mainstream cloud services such as Dropbox and Evernote, and a 'web clipping tool', which we'll be looking at in the very next chapter. If the worst comes to the worst and your Skype meeting falls apart, there is even a multiplayer game of battleships to help you settle any arguments!

TIP

Skype has a smartphone app for all major handsets that gives you all the benefits of VoIP calls when you're out and about with your mobile. Remember, you'll use up data when making a Skype call, which could cost you money if you're not on a WiFi connection.

viber.com

Skype may have the lion's share of VoIP traffic right now, but this is an up-and-coming technology sector with more companies climbing onto the voice-call gravy train all the time. Viber is a good choice if you prefer the indie option, offering voice calls, text and photo messaging between people who have the free smartphone app installed. There is no desktop computer version available, but all the major smartphone platforms are covered and you don't even need to register – just install the free app to connect with other Viber users instantly over WiFi or 3G mobile networks. It doesn't have quite the user base of Skype, but just a year after launch this fledgling VoIP service had clocked up over 50 million subscribers in 193 countries, and the company claims to be adding around 200,000 new sign-ups every day.

TIP

www.onavo.com
Get about five times more mobile surfing out of your data plan by installing Onavo Extend, a free app for iOS and Android that crunches data before it reaches your handset. Onavo Count is another app by the same people that helps you to keep track of your data usage, issuing alerts when you get close to data plan limits.

TEXTUALLY SPEAKING

Instant messaging for fast, convenient and free communication

An Ofcom study in 2011 found that we're now more likely to send a text message than pick up the phone. Texting makes perfect sense when you're busy at work because you can hold several conversations simultaneously over an extended period of time – and a text message doesn't need immediate attention in the same way as a phone call does, so it doesn't have to interrupt your work flow as much. Instant messenger apps are a great way to stay in touch through text messaging, as they use very little data and it is generally free to send and receive messages between users of similar services. There are loads of platforms to choose from and, like any social network, your choice will be mostly governed by what the people you want to talk to are using. Thankfully, a lot of the most popular platforms are now compatible with each other anyway, so you can communicate with your contacts no matter which service they have signed up to.

TIP

Find WiFi hotspots to jump onto when you're out and about with your smartphone. You'll find free apps on pretty well all smartphone platforms; just search for a term like 'free WiFi finder apps' to locate them. Google will also show the location of free WiFi in a city if you do a search on maps.google.com.

www.whatsapp.com

WhatsApp is a popular choice for straightforward, in-app messaging from person to person. It has one of the best ranges of supported platforms I've ever seen, available free on desktop machines of every flavour and across many mobile makes and models, including some non-smartphones. The interface is completely intuitive and when you first load it up you may be surprised by how many of your contacts are already using it.

TIP

www.opera.com/mobile
Smartphones all come with the manufacturer's preferred browser installed, but that doesn't make it the best one. Opera Mini renders and compresses websites, optimising them for mobile browsing and reducing the size by up to 90% before they are delivered to your handset – lowering the data usage and speeding up page delivery too.

www.ebuddy.com

Most of us will have contacts scattered across several instant messenger services, but that doesn't mean that you have to discard any of your friends. Chat platforms such as eBuddy let you collect a bunch of popular services together under one virtual roof, so you can see and interact with all your scattered contacts from the same central dashboard. Like WhatsApp, it supports an impressive range of devices, including desktop computers and mobile phones. It allows you to connect with people registered with many of the leading instant messenger services, including MSN, Yahoo!, Google Talk and Facebook.

imo.im

Another option, if you want to connect with lots of different chat services, is Imo – it's a newcomer to the crowd but that doesn't matter one jot, as it connects to 11 of the most popular instant messenger platforms today, including Facebook and Skype. As well as text messages you can send pictures, videos and even short voice messages (which is a little like using a walkie-talkie), and you can start group chats through the browser-based desktop interface or one of the free smartphone apps. I particularly like these apps, as they are fast and easy to use and connect with a huge number of my instant messenger contacts because of linking up with so many services.

TIP

With 1 billion users there is a pretty good chance that anyone you meet at a conference will have a Facebook account. Instead of giving them your phone number to make arrangements to meet up for dinner, why not connect through Facebook? You never really know what a person is going to be like until you spend a night out with them, and at least this way you can block them when you get home if they end up being a nightmare.

BACK TO BARTER

Reviving the ancient tradition of barter in a high-tech-trade environment

As hard as it is doing business today, the one thing you can be sure of is that you're not the only one feeling the pinch, so never be afraid of trying to strike a deal. There is a real revival in the concept of barter right now, making a mutually beneficial trade with one or more businesses for goods or services rather than cash. If you're a designer and you notice that your accountant has rubbish headed notepaper, why not offer to design them a new logo if they do your accounts free of charge? It can't hurt to ask and you could save yourself hundreds of pounds and gain a new customer to boot. Even if you don't have any special business skills, you can still dream up a good barter. If you're handy with a paintbrush and have some spare time, but no furniture in your new home office, offer to brighten up the front of an independent furniture shop in return for a desk and a set of shelving. It may seem obvious— or maybe you're embarrassed to strike up a conversation about saving money with a stranger? But it may surprise you to learn that more than 20% of world trade is believed to take place in non-monetary terms – in other words, by barter – and in today's economic climate there isn't a businessperson on the planet who wouldn't be interested in a good deal.

www.u-exchange.com

The social web is the perfect place for barter and multilateral trade communities to grow and blossom. As you'd expect, there are lots of them popping up all over the web, but among the biggest in the UK right now is U-Exchange. Free to sign up to and advertise your trade, there's no charge whatsoever for connecting you with other traders. You'll find people here offering everything from plumbing to photography, and in many cases they leave the trade item pretty open, inviting you to make them an offer depending on what skills you have personally. It's a brilliant system, and again you could be picking up a new long-term customer into the bargain. One word of warning: you should bear in mind that the website is self-regulated and you're paying nothing for the service, so there are no guarantees that you'll get quality products or services in your trade.

TIP

Doing a trade may feel like getting something for nothing because you're not paying any money, but you are still paying in 'time'. So, as with any business purchase or engaging someone's professional services, make sure that you check the trader's references and reputation before signing up.

hackerbuddy.com

Knowledge-trading websites are also a growing and very exciting trend on the web right now. A really good example is Hackerbuddy, which connects start-up businesses with programmers, designers and other webby types so that they can offer each other help and practical advice in their own specialist areas. The site is still fairly young but it is already home to a friendly and approachable community of more than 5,000 users. There is no charge for connecting you with another member, and if they accept your plea for help you are given each other's email addresses so that you can progress the project without the site's involvement. Remember, this service isn't supposed to replace hiring a professional to do a job, and abusing someone's time will get you nowhere – extremely fast. This community is all about mutual support and the occasional nod in the right direction.

MONEY MATTERS

Finance tools and accounting services

Arguably, one of the best ways to save money is simply knowing what's going on with it. Look after the pennies and the pounds will look after themselves is what they say, and who am I to argue with 'them'? Again, the Internet is awash with great tools and resources designed to streamline your accounting and help manage cash flow – are you getting bored of hearing me say that? When dealing with financial matters, I urge a lot more caution about what websites you trust with your data. Look for companies that have tight security and good customer services – a quick glance through their Facebook page or Twitter mentions should flag up any potential PR issues. And don't expect to get something amazing for nothing in this case – you are better off paying a couple of quid a week if the company is investing that money in keeping your information safe and secure. Ultimately, there is always the risk that your account could be compromised, and this applies to the web as a whole. You could also get pick-pocketed or your house could get burgled. I don't want to bring you down, but sometimes crappy stuff just happens. Just as crossing the road could result in your getting run over, so doing your banking online could result in your account being hacked. But as long as you and the service provider are adequately protected and you're not doing anything stupid or that attracts the specific attention of any would-be hackers, it is unlikely that you will become a direct victim.

It will naturally take some people longer to trust the Internet enough to do their banking online, and it's not for me to try to persuade you either way in this book (although I think you may be astonished by how much it changes your life being able to hop online any time of day or night to sort out your weekly finances). Banking aside, there are tools and services that will completely change the way you run your business, from purchasing stock right the way through to paying your tax in a couple of clicks. Nobody likes to think about tax, so, like a plaster, I find it's best to rip it off nice and fast.

www.moneydashboard.com

Keeping track of your money can become quite tedious if you have lots of credit cards and accounts, like most start-up businesses. Money Dashboard is one of a growing breed of 'account aggregators' that tap

135

into the information in your bank accounts and credit card companies (with your authorisation, of course) so that you can 'read' all that information through a central dashboard. You can add as many accounts and cards as you like, giving you a bird's-eye view of your finances in one place. Sounds convenient? Yes. Is it secure? Well, the site is as secure as you're going to get. All your bank logins are handled through a service called Yodlee, which is used by some of the biggest banks in America, so it has pretty tight security. The access you're granting is also 'read only', so while someone who broke in might be able to see how good or bad your finances were, they couldn't do anything to change them. There is also the small issue that some banks still don't like customers using an account aggregator, though they are becoming more acceptable as the technology proves itself to be secure. Once all your accounts are in the system you can set budgets and extract all manner of reporting and balance alerts. The company itself makes money through commission on sales of additional financial products, so expect to be sold to occasionally when using this free service.

TIP

You may have the occasional client who only wants to receive an invoice in the post. FreshBooks and many other services like this let you buy 'stamps' and will print out and mail your invoice in the traditional way for a few pence. Or you can download the PDF, print it out and post it yourself.

www.freshbooks.com

Like most normal human beings you hate having to do the accounts and sometimes even put off invoicing for such a long time that you forget how much to charge the customer (not just me, surely?). If that sounds anything like you, there is a revelation waiting online: automatic invoicing. Personally, I use FreshBooks, as I love the clear and unfussy interface and fantastic customer service, but there are lots of services springing up all the time, so you're best off looking at prices and services at the time of signing up. As with most sites like this, you get to try it out free for a month so that you can decide for yourself. If you normally shy away from this kind of thing because it sounds a nightmare to set up, think again. You have to add customers and jobs only once, which is no more complicated than typing out and emailing an invoice the way you do at the moment, I'll guarantee it. From that point on, raising an invoice is just a couple of clicks, sending it straight from the website once you've cleared it with your client. It looks after your paperwork from estimate to money in the bank, letting you offset expenses and manage contract work and time sheets all completely painlessly, with just a couple of clicks. There is even the option to activate electronic payments by PayPal and credit card, though there could be merchant charges involved that you should check up on first. And at the end of a tax period you can pull up all your accountant-friendly profit and loss statements and other normally quite terrifying paper-trail activities with a few clicks. Short, sharp – as I said earlier, just the way every sticking plaster should be dealt with. The addition of a free iPhone app (with hopefully the other smartphones covered soon, but I guess I shouldn't hold my breath) lets you do all this whenever you have a spare moment on the train or in a coffee shop, and means that you are much more likely actually to get all the tedious invoicing stuff done so that you can get on with the more serious job of reaping the profits. Just be aware of who is looking over your shoulder when you are doing anything with finances in public.

TIP

Sign up for the weekly reminder email that shows you in a clear pie chart and bar graphs exactly what you are owed, what you have spent, and, critically, what funds are overdue. This visual prompt has proved an effective nudge to do something I often avoid, which is chase up overdue invoices.

www.blinksale.com

Another popular online invoicing service is Blinksale. With many of the same features as FreshBooks, it's just going to come to price and service, plus whether you like using the dashboard. You get to decide for yourself with a free 15-day trial, after which there's a £10-a-month price tag for unlimited clients and invoices and plenty of automation and one-click conveniences to rival FreshBooks.

> ## ⌥ *TIP*
>
> *Both invoicing services can be fully integrated with a Basecamp account – the team-management hub we looked at in Chapter 4. Invoices can be generated straight from team members' logged hours, with no fiddly data entry on your part. You can even have the system send off an invoice automatically, if you're happy to trust it that much.*

www.expensify.com

Even if you're happy keeping your invoicing the way it's always been, surely I can tempt you to give over managing your expenses to the Internet? Why is it that we all hate doing expenses? Turning your receipts into cash, or even just a little off your tax bill, is a necessarily time-consuming and annoyingly fiddly job, so of course we put it off until we've lost half the receipts and forgotten what we bought with half of the rest. Expensify is a free smartphone app for every platform that lets you scan receipts with your phone's camera, then uses optical character recognition to run a 'smart scan' picking out details like currency, amount and supplier. It works pretty well if the receipt is printed clearly (which, of course, is not always the case). I say the app is free, but you get only 10 free smart scans a month, which unless you live an incredibly frugal life will never be enough. You can buy more credits – obviously one of the ways the company makes money – but you can also choose to enter receipt details by hand and continue to use the service free if you prefer. Once they are recorded, the website gives you lots of fantastic ways to manage and report on your expenses, even spitting out an accountant-friendly tax report at the end of the financial year.

1daylater.com

Another great expense-management and reporting tool is 1DayLater. The input form gives you set allocations, such as time, mileage, and expenses, all with drop-down menus, so it couldn't be quicker to fill out an entry. The colour-coding options for clients and jobs make the reporting page look nice and pretty, and for me the simple interface makes keeping track of finances and time a pleasure instead of a pain – something my long-suffering accountant will no doubt be thrilled about. There are also a few options for outputs, to which you get limited access for free, after which you'll need to pay a subscription to keep on using them. Altogether, a neat and easy-to-use ledger tool that should help to keep you in the money.

TIP

grndctrl.com
Grndctrl.com might not win any awards for complexity, or have the catchiest name in the world, but if you just want a quick and painless way to keep track of your finances and save for a specific target or goal, it offers exactly what you need – no more, no less – which I think must be the best way to handle austerity measures.

FAT-FREE BOTTOM LINE

With any luck, by now your business is looking lean and efficient, with a healthy bottom line. You've got your finances under control and you're ruling the balance sheet rather than it ruling you: no more hefty phone bills or outrageous office supplies orders. In fact, come to think of it, no more office to supply, either. You are now truly free to spend your money on the important things and let the cloud take care of the rest; like Dirty Harry walking off into the desert at sunset, guns smoking – metaphorically speaking, of course. If you're more of a Milky Bar Kid when it comes to trusting technology, it's OK to start with small steps – you may even be surprised at how quickly you pick up momentum and grow into Clint's dusty cowboy boots. Whether you're just starting out or run an established company that's struggling to swim upriver in these tight economic times, every stroke that you take towards saving money is going to make that swim a little bit easier. Stick with me, because now we've saved all that money the next chapter reveals some of the best *time*-saving features I've found on the Internet.

Chapter 7

Your cloud assistant

Managing your life and work with online tools and handy shortcuts

---

Everyone gets busy, but why is it that some people always seem to be busier than others? If that sounds like you, then this chapter is essential reading. You do want to become one of those annoying people, don't you? The ones who always seem to have time to enjoy a kick-about with their kids or make a family lasagne from scratch? In the coming pages we're going to get down to the nuts and bolts of running your life, and start shaving valuable time off your commitments to your business. From managing a busy diary to keeping track of social media streams and even fending off unwanted callers, there are lots of ways that the Internet can act as a buffer between you and time-wasting activities, taking mundane tasks off your hands and easing the stress of tracking work flow. In this chapter I'll be introducing you to your virtual assistant, exploring the myriad ways that cloud services can help to take the pain out of everyday operations, including:

- a virtual assistant at your beck and call 24/7
- managing and automating your tasks online
- productivity tools and time-saving tips for dealing with email
- finding and collecting useful information
- inside information tools for a competitive edge

- an interview with Doug Clark, IBM cloud expert
- ways to simplify your social activity and make it more effective
- social automation
- dos, don'ts and useful tools.

THE INTELLIGENT CLOUD

How smart is the Internet and could it really replace a human assistant?

We've all felt that we could use a personal assistant (PA) from time to time, but who can afford such a luxury these days? Luckily for those of us with a bottom line that can support only one salary, the Internet is prepared to work for free – and 24 hours a day. Before I get the PAs' union up in arms, I must stress that I'm not suggesting that web services are a good alternative to an *actual* human assistant. The Internet isn't yet capable of really understanding what we want in the same way as a person would. There's been a lot of amazing work done on artificial intelligence (AI) and the semantic web in recent years, though; which means, finding ways to make the Internet understand the nuances of human thought and language better, so that it can help us to find what we're really looking for. The price for this (you know you don't get something for nothing– right?) is that the Internet will also understand better how to sell stuff to us by learning our likes, dislikes and habits. Where you stand on privacy issues is your own choice. The head of leading technology firm Sun Microsystems said about 10 years ago: "You have zero privacy anyway, get over it." It was a controversial statement at the time, and privacy has remained a contentious issue to date. Aside from totally abstaining from the online world (which is pretty much unthinkable in this day and age), you can't avoid giving away some things about yourself. Personally, I don't see a problem in being advertised to if I'm getting useful services in return – and in many ways I'd rather see an advert for something I might find useful, if I have to see any at all.

TIP

Voice recognition technology has come on in leaps and bounds in the past year, so if you're not using the AI assistant on your smartphone you may want to think again. With these virtual assistants you can ask to be reminded to pick up your dry cleaning when you pass the shop and a location-based tag will be put on that task, triggering an alert when you get within range of the shop.

While the web isn't yet truly intelligent, it's starting to do a pretty good job of faking it. Artificial intelligence bots have been answering customer services queries for years on the web and, as we discussed earlier in this book, things like recommendation engines and personalised search services are beginning to make our machines respond to us in a much more human way. Web services are getting better at learning what we like and recognising patterns in wider human behaviour in order to make some smart assumptions about what we might really want to achieve. This kind of technology has been put to great use in making productivity aids. With voice recognition now improving to the point where you can hold a halfway decent conversation with your phone or desktop machine, it can really feel as if you're interacting with an intelligent being. It took me about six months to stop saying 'thank you' to my smartphone after asking it to turn the alarm clock on at the end of the evening; and when I did eventually notice that I had stopped saying 'thank you' I have to confess that it made me stop and wonder momentarily about the state of my moral compass.

 TIP

To activate a free PA on your smartphone, iPhone users get Siri installed as standard and Android users can download a good free alternative app called Evi. As well as reminding you to pick up your suits from the dry cleaner's, they will do things like reminding you about deadlines, searching the Internet, dialling up numbers and telling you what the weather will be like on Friday.

LOTS OF LISTS

A task manager to suit every need

I've become a bit of a list person; it's the only way to keep on top of everything when you're juggling several contracts. But have you ever felt overwhelmed, as you scan through your list, by the number of upcoming deadlines? List managers are all about filtering out the noise so that you can give 100% to the job at hand without being distracted by the future. There are lots of them popping up on the web right now, with dozens of different twists and dimensions on the same basic principle: managing your to-do list. It's important to choose a service that's simple — a list is designed to make your life easier, not more complicated, after all. I've picked out a few of my favourites to give you an idea of what's out there.

www.nozbe.com

Nozbe is an organisational hub for you and your team that lets you share lists and tasks from whatever smartphone or desktop platform you're using. The apps even work offline, so if your connection drops you still know what you need to do. The concept here is very simple: start a project, then add scheduled tasks, inviting collaborators to interact with the lists alongside you. Collaborators can add comments and updates to the tasks, like a simple noticeboard attached to each thread. One of the intelligent time-saving features here is the ability to add context to each task. You get only five projects and five contexts to play with in the free account (and 1MB of storage) but if you find it useful enough to want more there are various monthly subscriptions you can upgrade to. A context could be where you need to be in order to complete a task, such as at home on your computer or on your mobile in town. So next time you have half an hour to spare in town, Nozbe will let you know straight away what you could be doing to use that time productively, without cluttering your mind with all the things you can't do right now anyway. It also integrates with a few popular online tools that we've already mentioned — like Twitter, Google Calendar, Dropbox and Evernote, which is a note-taking and research tool that you may have seen a lot already as you browse the web and that we're finally going to be talking about later in this chapter.

TIP

Collaborators whom you invite will need to register an account with Nozbe before being able to interact with your project. Make sure that you get permission before giving anyone's email address to an online service, as many people (quite rightly) object to this invasion of their privacy. Alternatively, you can make your project public and just share the web page with them to view your list.

www.nirvanahq.com

Nirvana is much the same, although the interface looks a little more business-like. As with Nozbe, you can group your tasks into projects and invite collaborators to interact with you through comments and updates. There are no limits here on projects or contexts, which in this case are just simple 'responsibility' labels that you can set up however you like. Everything here is free to use, though you're limited as to platform, with only browser access and iPhones currently supported. To compensate, it gives you a personal email address to use if you want to add tasks on the fly. You can also set a to-do list to be emailed to you on designated days, keeping the mental clutter to a minimum – just the way I like it. Another nice addition is the ability to categorise tasks based on how much energy they will require, so you can dial up a list of things to do that suits a particular mood.

 TIP

cantyouseeimbusy.com
Remember to take a two-minute brain-break every so often. At Can't You See I'm Busy! there's a collection of iconic arcade games that from a distance look like you're just working on a spreadsheet or word-processing document. My favourite is playing Pong by destroying the words in a document. A fantastic way to take a break without anyone noticing you're slacking off!

www.any.do

One last task manager I want to show you has been around as a smartphone app for a while and has now made itself available through a browser in the form of a Chrome add-on, with a web app promised soon as well. It hooks up with Facebook, so no need for a new account, and this makes sharing a natural part of the experience too. This app definitely works on the premise that less is more when it comes to lists, and I'm inclined to agree – they are a necessary evil of a busy life and the last thing we need to do is clutter them up. The app is more fun to use on the smartphone, with voice recognition note-taking and just a few taps to set reminders and attach folders for sharing with other people. All this is provided free of charge, so you can see for yourself if it is the right task manager for you.

 TIP

www.usetrackthis.com
If you're sending a package with any of the leading parcel delivery services, have TrackThis act as your personal assistant by tracking the delivery for you, reporting to you proactively in the form of a tweet, email or text message when it reaches its destination safely.

EMAIL MANIA

Time-saving tips for dealing with email

It's reckoned that the average corporate email user deals with 105 messages a day, and despite the use of spam filters about 19% of them will still be junk emails. According to a 2012 report, spammers cost society $20 billion a year, making only $200 million of revenue in the process. It's a problem we just haven't been able to solve on the web, and will no doubt be a major cause of the ultimate demise of old-fashioned email in favour of more dynamic communication streams through social media and cloud platforms. It's believed that this could save people up to a third of the working day, but with an estimated 3 billion users globally (that's three times the size of Facebook's user base), email is going to be hard to kill off entirely. There are ways in which you can cut out the clutter of dealing with your inbox though, freeing up time to do something more productive. Here are a few simple tactics for the ruthlessly efficient emailer.

- **Set a time limit:** don't succumb to the temptation of checking your emails every time you need a break from whatever it is you're concentrating on; it is counterproductive to force your mind to keep changing lanes throughout the day. Instead, set yourself a couple of 15-minute blocks each day to deal with all your emails at once – and if you really do need a break, step away from your computer and get some fresh air.
- **Get your priorities right:** most email packages have a flagging system, enabling you to mark incoming messages based on how urgently they must be dealt with. Get used to using these flags and you'll save time, filtering out the noise when you are busy. And don't be afraid to bin unsolicited messages that are of no benefit to your business, without sending a reply.
- **Don't over complicate it:** there is a good chance that a lot of the emails you deal with each day require a variation on the same 5 or 10 replies, but do you still write a personal reply to each customer anyway? Save your time and theirs by creating short, succinct reply templates for every occasion that you can fire off; or better yet, direct queries towards your social networks so that you can keep them updated whilst building a good customer bond.
- **Get over the archiving obsession:** it's good to keep certain messages for future reference, but if an email just contains a comment like "OK, thanks for the reply", don't waste time thinking about where the right folder for it is. Just hit the delete button and move on.
- **Know when to say goodbye:** email is generally a very reactive tool – someone sends you a message so you reply, and so the ping-pong match goes on. But do you really need to get caught up in a never-ending string of goodbyes? When the topic of an email has been dealt with, archive it or delete it and get on with something useful.

146

TIP

inboxzero.com/video
There's a very good blog called 43 Folders that covers productivity tips and tools from a creative perspective. The writer has posted a collection of ideas and articles called 'Zero Inbox' and it is well worth a read if you struggle to keep on top of email – alternatively, watch the thought-provoking video lecture on this link.

inboxpause.com

It's not always possible to completely clear your inbox, but if you let too many messages stack up it can become unmanageable to filter by eye, not to mention depressing being reminded of all the emails you haven't got round to dealing with yet. If you're using Gmail there is an answer to stem the flow: INBOX PAUSE is a Chrome browser add-on that hides any new messages away where they can't bother you until you have dealt with what is already on your plate. You can set it up to send an auto reply to any messages that you put on hold – perhaps suggesting that the sender contact you via another means of communication if it's urgent – until you have worked your way through the backlog. Having the chance to pause and concentrate on the job in hand before being distracted by another email should make it much easier to deal with your workload efficiently.

TIP

www.emailcharter.org
Studies have shown that it takes longer to respond to an email than it takes to create it, so make sure you don't commit any digital faux pas by reading up on the Email Charter. It lists 10 essential tips for anyone who doesn't want to annoy their friends and colleagues with excessive email missives.

www.baydin.com

Another very useful email add-on is Boomerang from Baydin. It lets you send messages back out into the ether, to be redelivered to your inbox at a time when you can handle them – saving that dreaded bulge as the inbox fills up with non-time-critical communications. The Gmail extension for Chrome and Firefox is free to install and use and there is a 30-day free trial if you want to add it to your desktop version of Outlook.

TIP

www.royalmail.com/discounts-payment/smartstamp
When you occasionally have to send 'snail mail', in other words an ordinary letter dropped in a post box, create a good impression by dressing it up like a fancy corporation with Smart Stamps – an online service from the Royal Mail that lets you print postage directly onto an envelope, together with your own logo or graphics.

WHAT? WHEN? HOW?

Productivity tools with different perspectives on your life

www.sunrise.im

A good PA will have a list of the day's appointments and tasks all clearly mapped out by the time you arrive for work in the morning – and a really good PA will have placed your agenda beside a steaming cappuccino. The Internet can't do the coffee (yet), but Sunrise fulfils the main objective with a daily digest of everything you need to know about the day ahead pulled from all your key communications streams. Sign up to connect with Facebook, multiple Google accounts and LinkedIn. As well as your calendar you can add other features for the digest to include, like public holidays, or birthdays pulled from Facebook contacts. When you accept an invitation in Facebook it will automatically be synced to your account, and that goes for all the separate Google calendars that you might be running for business and personal commitments too.

If you have a meeting with a LinkedIn contact you will also receive a summary of their details, together with their profile photograph. You will never be better prepared for a business meeting – just try not to know so much that it looks creepy.

rescuetime.com

The Internet can be a great productivity aid, but it can also be a massive time sink if you're easily distracted. If you're likely to fall victim to procrastination when you're online, RescueTime wants to come to your rescue. After downloading and installation, the application will help you to monitor, track and control your Internet usage – collecting data and providing detailed reports on what you did, where you did it and how productive it was. There's a free version for private use, and if you upgrade to the paid subscription you can ask the software to block you (or your staff) from unproductive websites when they are used excessively. It can also send you an alert when anyone is wasting too much time online – *1984* anyone? Whether you're running a small office or working alone at home, it makes a very good reality checker. With RescueTime looking over your shoulder there is little chance that you'll be asking yourself "Where did the day go?" You'll have a graph and several pie charts telling you exactly where it went – kind of like procrastination. Whether you have the strength of mind to act upon those findings is another matter entirely.

www.veodin.com/keyrocket

If you've ever watched someone on a computer who seems to be working incredibly fast it's most likely because they are using keyboard shortcuts. This involves pressing a certain combination of keys to execute a complicated task at a stroke – tasks like making a new folder or returning to the desktop, which would otherwise have taken two or three seconds of mouse clicking to complete. You may think life is too short to be memorising all the keyboard shortcuts for your operating system – and you'd be right. But learning a couple of strategic ones that will really benefit your work flow could be the biggest time-saver you make all year. Once installed, KeyRocket will watch how you use your computer and come up with a few killer key combinations that your life is really too short NOT to learn, as they will save you so much time overall. It will slow you up a little to begin with, as the app will occasionally interrupt your work to prompt you to use that keyboard shortcut instead of mouse click-click-clicking. It's a touch annoying when you're working hard, but once you learn to use the shortcut you will have formed a valuable time-saving habit. With your most common actions covered, KeyRocket will continue to pop up keyboard shortcut suggestions from your system tray – if you want to be prompted to learn one of them click the heart, or the bin if you don't want to see it again.

RESEARCH ASSISTANT

Tools to help you find and collect useful information

When I interviewed Theo Paphitis in Chapter 2, one of the points he stressed was the need to do your research when setting up a business. If knowledge really is power, as Theo said, you have an army of foot soldiers waiting online to sniff it out and gather it up on your behalf. Web-clipping tools and aggregators are everywhere online right now. I use these terms to loosely describe the slew of web gadgets and browser add-ons that make it easier to find and remember stuff online. They are abundant, and with good reason because the information they have to sift through and organise for you is beyond abundant many millions of times over. We've already spoken in terms of 8 billion plus indexed pages. These information-sorting apps can also be pretty 'quick and dirty' to make if you know anything about programming web services, because they are essentially just riffling through and presenting other people's content rather than making any original content themselves. That is not to underplay their importance to the web experience, though, as long as they are done well. It's pretty much the only way you could hope to make sense of the expanding vastness of the Internet right now.

www.news.me

Information bombards us from every direction online. People love to share, and the mass connectivity of social media means that very popular stories are likely to hit your incoming social feeds like a swarm of vaguely interesting bees. News.me wants to be your trivial information riot shield, filtering out the noise to deliver an easy-to-manage digest of the important posts coming from your busiest social streams. Sign up with email or download the free iPhone app, authorise access to your Twitter and Facebook accounts, then just sit back and let the app email you every morning with a summary of the day's posts from your network.

flipboard.com
If you have one of the popular tablet computers – iPad, Android, Kindle Fire or NOOK – Flipboard is not only a convenient way to catch up on recent posting activity in your news and social streams, it looks and feels gorgeous to use. It's not even that bad on the smaller smartphone screens, though the true magazine-style page turning and crisp, modern presentation are definitely more rewarding on the larger, high-definition screens. You can fill these pages with stories from news websites, blogs, social channels and loads of other pre-linked websites and services, making it all very easy to put together. Not bad for a free app that helps you to stay in touch stylishly without cluttering up your desktop.

CLOUD CLIPPINGS

Web tools for note-taking and saving information for later
One of the things you'll notice when you start to surf the web more freely is how easy it is to lose things. I'm forever thinking to myself "Where was that great picture or story?" It's a sad truth that I have even been known to lose a piece of software on my computer – knowing what it does but being unable to recall the name of it. In my defence, I must say that I download an awful lot of bits of software to try out for review, but I've been able to improve my web memory by using a clipping tool. This is another heavily populated area when it comes to service providers online. Most work on the freemium model, the basic services being free, with micropayment upgrades for things like more storage or organisational features.

www.evernote.com
You can't really talk about web-clipping tools without talking about Evernote. The granddaddy of the genre, it now has around 35 million users, and free apps for all the major desktop and mobile platforms. It lets you grab whole web pages or just a bit of one, take notes, capture audio and photos and organise those snippets of your life so that they can

be accessed again anywhere, from any device. It's like having someone standing behind you with a notepad that you can just turn to and say "Oh, remind me about that when I'm looking for it later, would you?" The basics are free, with a reasonably generous 2GB of free storage, and the prices for upgrading are competitive if you want to make Evernote your main cloud storage drive. This has added benefits because of the number of fantastic tools and services that have Evernote integration built in, making linking up two independent resources as simple as clicking a button. We've already seen several examples of this in these chapters, including IQTELL, which appeared in Chapter 4. Evernote itself has also developed an impressive stable of add-ons, some free and some not. Check the icons on the homepage for more – they include apps like Skitch for adding annotations, symbols and sketches to the world around you; or Hello, which helps you to remember the people you meet by letting you create a searchable history of people, connections and shared experiences.

TIP

Web-clipping tools will generally have a button somewhere that you can drag onto your browser toolbar to automatically send pages that you're currently looking at to your clippings folder.

springpad.com

Springpad is another freemium web clipper that offers similar features to Evernote, with the ability to clip and store information synced across a variety of different formats – and the apps for Android and iPhone even let you scan a product barcode, which is great if you're out at the shops and want to check if something is available cheaper online when you get home. You can organise and sort your notes really simply, with an events diary and task list built in – plus, it being location aware, you can make a note of all those great restaurants and useful little places that you stumble upon out of the blue and never seem to be able to find again. As well as storing notes, the website pulls data from other available sources, helping you to add context to your notes and act on them more easily – for example, items can be added to your weekly shopping list just by entering the URL of a recipe that you want to cook.

> **TIP**
>
> *Link your web-clipping service to your social media accounts, like Facebook and Twitter, to make sharing the information you save really simple and organic.*

www.memonic.com

One of the criticisms levelled at cloud note-takers like this is how many useless pixels they are on your screen if you can't connect to the Internet. It's a fair point, and one that Memonic overcomes with a free offline mode for its browser plug-in and Android and Apple mobile apps (something for which you have to pay a premium upgrade in other popular apps right now). It's the service's unique selling point, because otherwise it does pretty much the same as Evernote and Springpad. As with all of these things, you're better off giving them all a try before you decide which one best suits your needs.

gimmebar.com

Another tool to pop in your 'oh, that's useful' box is Gimme Bar– a place to save all those interesting snippets that you come across but that also lets you back up your social media messages to a Dropbox folder. Possible backups include Instagram and Twitter. The clipping tool also works quite nicely, creating a 'drop zone' at the bottom of your browser where you can just drag and drop images and chunks of text off a website to save them in different categories.

INFORMATION BLOODHOUNDS

Proactive research tools to keep you on top of the web

trap.it

Storing information is only part of the battle – you have to find it first, and with the web changing so rapidly it is impossible for one person to stay on top of things. Believe me, I've spent the last 10 years researching this. But you don't have to take the strain of finding all the latest content on your own shoulders, as there are plenty of intelligent discovery tools aching to be by your side. Tools like Trapit, which lets you build a 'trap' around a particular subject which it will then diligently keep updated with all the latest news and posts on the topic, stashing anything interesting in your feed so you can catch up with it when you have time. If you give the site some feedback, saying which links were useful and which were not, it will continue learning about what you like, making the content it suggests ever more focused to your taste. Trapped articles are delivered in a nice-looking interface that uses a very 'now' boxes design with integrated sharing through Twitter and Facebook.

A MAN ON THE INSIDE

Web services and tools that give you an edge

Digital technology has completely changed the way we communicate, making it possible to send messages anywhere in the world free of charge – and in most cases the message should arrive just a few moments after you've sent it. The downside of this immediacy is that letters are no longer as special as they used to be. Emails are so easy to send that the receiver is often completely overwhelmed with spam and unsolicited sales messages, so it can be next to impossible to make them pay attention if you're not already in their network of trusted contacts. Advances in technology also mean that it's much easier for con artists to set up a website and try to dupe you, but you can take a few simple precautions against these common pitfalls.

whois.domaintools.com

Know who you're dealing with right off the bat with the WHOIS domain tools, which will show you who owns a domain name, with company address and contact details. Some people can pay to opt out of having their personal details listed on this database but they have to register their site through an umbrella company instead. This is fine for individuals who perhaps don't want to get random phone calls to their personal mobile number – but I would be very suspicious of any supposedly large corporation website that doesn't have complete transparency about its registered company details.

www.duedil.com

For deeper information about every company in the UK and Ireland and its directors, Duedil reveals the hidden story based on a combination of public records and 900 news website feeds. The service queries 10 billion pieces of information on everything from litigation to financial results. The numbers are presented in an easily digestible format that comes complete with 'red flags' to help you steer clear of obvious bad apples. The website now has over 8.6 million company profiles in its database and the service is expanding rapidly, with more than 400,000 downloads a week. With so many businesses teetering on the brink of ruin in these tough economic times, this could be the advanced warning you need to prevent your getting into bed with a struggling company. You can do a basic search on company name and location without registering, with the option to register a free account for even more detailed reports and data. The site is quite new but it is also encouraging users to rate and comment on companies they know, thus building a bank of human opinion to complement the official data.

www.surveymonkey.com

If you really want to keep your customers happy, the best thing you can do is ask them how. Whether you're deciding on flavours for next week's soup of the day, or choosing a design for your new website, the simple act of asking your customers' opinions will build a lot of loyalty: they feel invested in the outcome and you are giving them another reason to keep interacting with your social stream, so you won't slip under their radar. SurveyMonkey is an elegant solution for garnering the opinions of your crowd. The free plan lets you set 10 questions with up to 100 respondents to each — and if you want any more than that there are premium upgrades, currently starting at £24 a month.

TIP

www.rmonline.com/armadillo-app.html
aRMadillo is a free smartphone app on Android, Apple and BlackBerry that lets you perform a quick search for a company's credit report. There are premium reports that you can download for a price and they are worth getting if you're looking at making a substantial investment, but the free search should give you an initial perception of whether you should worry about a company's financial health.

oneleap.to

Sometimes getting your ideas in front of the right people can be a huge mountain to climb. People are bombarded with sales messages and pitches all day long, especially those with the power and influence to do business with you. OneLeap is a new concept that's hoping to put some value back into email by asking the sender to make a cash deposit against their belief that it's a message the recipient will want to read. This is a very new idea and is still a little conceptual. Investors, influencers and all kinds of business people have signed up, describing on their profile the kinds of things they are interested in hearing about. At the time of writing, the service was open to sign up to as a sender or a receiver, but the developers tell me that they will soon be making it 'invitation only' for a period, so as to ensure that the right kind of network is built. If it's still closed and you pass the criteria to join, it will be well worth having a browse through the profiles, as the descriptions may spark an idea based on your own skills and knowledge. If you want to contact someone there will be a fee – set by the recipient. I've seen this range from $8 to $240, though for the most part contacting a high-level executive seems to be around $20–$30 (and this is one good reason, the developers tell me, why they want to open the doors to invitations only, so that the price of high-level executives can be made more affordable to genuine entrepreneurs). You will get a guaranteed reply to your email within 10 days, otherwise your account will be refunded. When you do receive a reply, 80% of your fee goes to a nominated charity, and of course the other 20% is the way the site makes money. I don't normally recommend stuff where you have to pay, but I do really like this idea: $30 is nothing if you're getting your business plan or proposal read seriously by someone who can actually help to make it happen, and I can't deny a bit of extra charity funding goes a long way. You can also set a subject and amount for which you would consider 'selling a reply for charity'– whether anyone will take you up on that offer is another matter entirely, but since it will cost you nothing and your favoured charity could benefit, what exactly have you got to lose?

Profile

Doug Clark, IBM Cloud Computing Leader

"If someone tells you 'no, this cannot be done', you should always query that and see it as an opportunity to make a success out of something that no one else is doing."

Doug Clark really understands the importance of taking advantage of cloud technologies for businesses of any size. He heads up IBM's Cloud Computing division for the UK and Ireland, pulling together the best cloud skills and technologies that IBM has to offer and finding ways to apply them to the everyday needs and challenges of its clients, and he is very much an evangelist on the subject. Doug studied biochemistry at university but discovered an aptitude for business communications and networking when he got involved in helping to run university societies. Following a stint in sales and marketing for the pharmaceutical industry after graduation, he ended up running a global pharma brand as a product manager. It was during this stage of his career that he realised the importance of change and developed his skills in helping to effect it, despite often strong resistance from the business community. As a result he was instrumental in changing a major prescription drug into an over-the-counter drug, now available in supermarkets around the world. Next he joined the PricewaterhouseCoopers consulting group, which was acquired by IBM in 2002. Doug went with the sale, beginning a phase of his career that he describes as "one of the most exciting seat-of-the-pants rides I've ever had in business".

Doug said:
Change is so important in business, but so many people resist it, even though it is often futile to do so. When I was trying to move a drug from being a prescription drug to being an over-the-counter drug, I was told by people both within my

organisation and externally that it was impossible. But I did achieve it in the end, so one of my early lessons was always to query the word 'no' because something that is comparatively unloved could actually turn into a pot of gold for an organisation. That, in a nutshell, is the idea I have built most of my career on. I call it 'intrapreneurism', because I've usually worked within an enterprise or organisation bringing relatively immature ideas successfully to market. Cloud technologies have been maturing very rapidly and are really exciting for small businesses as they can 'play' like much bigger companies – I think of it like David versus Goliath. They can get into cloud in a really inexpensive, low-risk way, dabbling in new ideas until they have a proven business model they can then start to scale up very rapidly. It means small businesses don't have to plough all their seed funding and start-up capital into technology resources – and bigger organisations like IBM are constantly trying to behave more like small, nimble organisations, so cloud is beneficial to the big guys too because it allows them to operate in a more agile way. I don't think it's possible to survive in business today without embracing cloud technology; if you try to postpone the inevitable what you risk doing is giving your competitors an unfair advantage. Like everything in life, practice makes perfect and I would say it's the same for working with the Internet. But don't fall into the trap of thinking there is a 'free lunch' out there. Everything comes at a price and with cloud technology that price might be giving up some of your privacy, or making yourself more vulnerable. So my advice is, keep your eyes wide open and your feet on the ground, and don't feel like you always have to be at the bleeding edge of your business. Sometimes it's better to be number two and let someone else take the 'scar tissue' – and if someone tells you 'no, this cannot be done', you should always query that and see it as an opportunity to make a success out of something that no one else is doing.

www.ibm.com/cloud-computing/us/en

(For the IBM UK small- and medium-sized enterprise site: www.ibm.com /midmarket/uk/en)

IBM is probably best known for working with huge global enterprises, but it actually spans the entire portfolio of customers, right down to small, three- or four-person operations, offering support and advice on every aspect of cloud computing. You can find out more about its services on the midsize pages of its website, including free business advice in its 'Knowledge Hub'. One of the initiatives Doug is keen to promote is finding smaller, developer-type organisations to embed with IBM partners, giving them access to IBM hardware and software services for the purpose of mutual support and learning. You can make your own application for one of these partnerships on its website.

SOCIAL ASSISTANTS

Ways to simplify your social activity and make it more effective

Real assistant?

When you start getting serious about social media it could be very time consuming. If you have good reason to believe that the time you're dedicating to it is translating into actual profit, it may be time to think about hiring a professional. They are likely to be much more efficient than you because they don't have a million other things to worry about – and if you choose wisely they should have some great ideas of their own to bring to the table. You can hire social media experts by the day, hour or just to help out with a particular campaign if you prefer – though, obviously, committing longer term to an individual should put you in a stronger position both emotionally and financially. The key thing to remember is that you are hiring someone to speak directly to the public on your behalf, so they have to be a good personality fit too. You can use the recruitment tools that we spoke about in Chapter 4 as a starting point, but ask around within your networks for recommendations too – if your customers already know and like a social media manager from another campaign, that has to be a pretty solid starting point.

TIP

Nowhere will you find out more about a social media expert than in their own social media channels, so make sure that you do a healthy amount of snooping before engaging anyone to speak on behalf of your brand. If they do not have a reasonably long and positive social presence, think again about who you hire.

Virtual assistant?

If your bottom line can't support another hungry mouth (or you'd just rather keep your money in your pocket and let the Internet take some of the slack) there are some great social automation tools that you can bring into your work flow – but these recommendations come with a warning and a possible price to pay. The debate about whether it is right, or even ethical, to use automation tools in a so-called 'social' environment has raged good and strong for several years now. Some say that these tools, which let you schedule ongoing interactions with any number of social networks without having to lift a finger once they have been set up, will end up being the 'spam email' of the social web, eventually cheapening the incoming data stream to such a degree that it gets killed off as meaningful communication. Personally, I think there are certain things that it is completely acceptable to automate. For example, in running the BBC *Click* Twitter account (@BBCClick) I have a few automatic posts to remind people of the broadcast times over the weekend and inviting them to come and discuss the stories on Facebook and Google Plus. It means that I don't have to be glued to the computer all weekend – and I don't think our viewers mind that it's an automated message. You might also be launching a promotion on a particular day but have an hour to spare for setting it up a few days before. Automating that post to happen when your head is inside the project will save you having to switch lanes a few days later when it pops up in your diary again. What you must never do is abuse your social streams with endless robotic posts and sales spam; and don't ever kid yourself that repeated automated marketing posts look like anything other than what they are: soulless pieces of information delivered without any of the benefits of the social web.

TIP

You don't have to stay at your desk late at night in order to reach the decent-sized social audiences. Find out which are the busiest times on the networks that you like posting to and use automation tools to schedule that day's tweets for the times when they are most likely to be seen.

bufferapp.com

For those auto-posts that you can justify, Buffer is a really nice and simple solution. It handles LinkedIn and Facebook brand pages as well as personal profiles, plus Twitter and a pretty obscure social channel called App.net (you probably won't have heard of that one because of the $50 price tag). Once signed up, you add the days and times when you want to post stuff, and then everything you drag into the Buffer drop zone will be added to your queue. It's a simple and elegant way of mapping out your social posts and then just filling in the content as things pop up. The site will even suggest a post – some kind of motivational quote pulled off the Internet – if you're desperate for ideas; but use too many and you are likely to end up looking a bit desperate too. There are simple analytics telling you how many people you may have reached and a little about how your message was received. A free app for iPhone rounds off this offering – and hopefully other smartphone platforms may be supported in the future too.

TIP

Remember Tweriod back in Chapter 2 – the tool that analyses your account to tell you the best time to make a post? You can link to this service and Buffer will automatically use the best time to schedule your tweets on it, constantly updating data – so you can always be sure that your tweets are most effective.

TIP

Get your customers and readers to be your automation tools by adding social media sharing buttons and links to any content that you post online. All of the blogging platforms and website-building tools we have spoken about in this book will let you add these features inside the content-management dashboard.

sendible.com

Fire up the Sendible social dashboard and you get a completely different feeling; where Buffer is a sleek and elegant place to drop your ideas, Sendible looks like it wants to sit you down in a swivel chair and bore you to death with spreadsheet equations. This is a tool for the serious socialite and there is a price tag attached to prove it, with a 30-day free trial before you have to hand over your credit card for anything from £10 to £500 a month. If you do sign up you'll get a lot more power and control for the investment, with deeper analytics and more complex scheduling options. Depending on the subscription you choose, you can run anywhere from 15 social streams upwards, even sending out SMS messages and bulk emails, which is perfect if you have people signing up for a newsletter – but again, never become a spammer by sending unsolicited sales messages en masse. Both iPhone and Android users have the option of an app as well, so you can post on the go.

TIP

roundteam.co
If you want to share links and news on a particular subject, you can set up RoundTeam to look for hashtags and usernames, retweeting anything it finds on your behalf. Be careful using this, as the app just looks at key words, which can have very different meanings depending on the context.

TIME ON YOUR HANDS

A quiet revolution in 'a little more me time'

I hope that this chapter has freed up a little more of your time – time you could spend playing football with the children or making lasagne, or drumming up even more business, and so the cycle of life goes on. There is certainly plenty on the Internet that you can find to fritter that time away if you're at a loose end, but I'm not going to let us get distracted at this stage of the game; with just a few more chapters to go, let's press ahead (and if you really want to waste some time online, come and have a chat to me on Twitter!). But I have plenty more in store yet; and with all this talk about saving money and making more time we haven't even touched on one of the most exciting dynamics of the brand new connected world: how to make money online. We'll be taking that journey in Chapter 10, but first we'll be having a riffle through my virtual briefcase, picking over all the interesting curiosities I've gathered on my travels that don't seem to fit anywhere else – but you definitely can't afford to leave out.

 TIP

ifttt.com
This is a fantastic automation tool that lets you create 'recipes' that automate complex activities between two different social channels. For example, you could set up a recipe to post any @ mentions of you on Twitter to your Facebook brand page timeline. There are pre-made recipes for practically every occasion and dozens of the most popular social tools are supported.

Chapter 8

Inside my virtual briefcase

Little pieces of web brilliance that didn't fit anywhere else

No matter how organised you try to be, there are always things around your desk that just don't fit anywhere sensible – those useful tools that you use all the time and want to keep handy, but by themselves are not worth labelling a whole shelf for. I'm hoping that that sentiment rings true with more people than just me, because that is where we're going throughout Chapter 8. For me, those little desktop extras end up in my briefcase, itself a relic from the 1990s that gathers dust under the printer table because these days I can fit everything I need for a hundred meetings on just one tablet computer. My real briefcase contains some fairly mundane stuff: a hole punch, though I can't remember the last time I needed to punch a hole in anything; a tape dispenser that makes a couple of cameos a year for birthdays, with a starring role at Christmas; assorted mobile phone chargers and a big, tangled mess of cable – did you really expect anything else? My *virtual* briefcase, however, is a lot more interesting. This chapter contains an assortment of uncategorised digital gifts and gadgets that you never knew you needed, until right now. These include:

- tips and tools to cut down on stationery
- the bare essentials for keeping your data safe
- smart password security tips and tools

- making presentations and promotional films that will really impress
- interview with serial entrepreneur and founder of Enterprisenation.com Emma Jones
- tools and tips for making short work of sharing content and other everyday tasks
- taking your office in your pocket with a portable cloud.

PAPER STACKS

Stationery-busting tools and resources to reduce the paper you use

We'll start with the stuff you might find useful around the office – especially if you're looking to cut down on stationery or even go completely paperless. As well as being good for your pocket and the environment, getting rid of paper makes tracking your administration and generating reports a lot easier (of course, if you were paying attention through the previous chapters this is something you will know already). No more digging through a dozen fat files looking for one tiny slip of paper – in the digital office it's there at your fingertips in just a few clicks. Who wouldn't see the merits? But the truth is that going completely paperless is a big commitment, and a time sink initially while you set it all up and get everyone used to using it properly. It's also a fairly progressive work ethic, so you may have to compromise when dealing with some people. There are reams of reading on the topic of going paperless online (pun most definitely intended), and I think it's the way everyone will lean in the near future. But you don't have to go all out to start making serious savings on your stationery bill, so to get you going I've picked out a couple of tools you can start using straight away.

www.bullzip.com

When sending things like invoices and estimates via email it is better to save them in a file format that is not easy to edit, making it harder for anyone to try to pull a fast one by changing your numbers. PDFs are the accepted norm for this, as the software to read them is free and pretty much everyone has it installed because it comes bundled with so many other applications. You can make a basic PDF in Microsoft Word (just choose to 'save as' and select .pdf from the drop-down menu under 'file name'), but if you want more features and controls Bullzip has a free PDF printer that will write a .pdf document from virtually any Microsoft application. You can add things like password protection or a watermark to your documents for added security. You'll notice that on its homepage Bullzip lists a number of other applications you can download. You probably won't understand what to do with most of them – I barely do myself, to be honest – but the PDF-to-Word converter next to the PDF printer has self-explanatory benefits, should you ever want to edit a PDF document someone has sent you.

getsigneasy.com

Adding signatures to digital documents can be done in a number of ways. You can sign a piece of blank paper and then scan it into your computer and save it as an image file to embed at the end of a document. If you have a graphics tablet you can draw your signature in an image editor, like Photoshop or GIMP. SignEasy offers a much more elegant solution in the form of Apple and Android apps. Once you've set up your signature you can add it to any document by emailing yourself the PDF, then on your smartphone click and hold that email to choose 'open with SignEasy'. Now you can just drop the signature in the right place and save as a new document. You get only three credits to try the app out, after which there is a pay-as-you-go option, currently set a £1.49 for five documents. For a £6.99 premium upgrade you can add more signatures to unlimited documents and can add Dropbox, Box (another popular online drive) and Evernote integration to bring in your documents.

TIP

There are lots of scanner apps for smartphones of every flavour that will let you take a photograph of a document and turn it into a PDF document. You will probably have to pay a couple of quid to get a decent one – I use Scanner Pro on my iPhone, but only because I've had it for years.

CLOUD SAFETY

The bare essentials for keeping your data safe online

Talking about cloud security properly would take more than several chapters alone, and to be honest a paper book is not the best place to do this because of the ever-changing nature of the web. For every new advance we see online there are brand new dangers unleashed – but that's not an excuse to lock down your hatches and refuse to take advantage of the benefits of being online. As scary as all the stories are about viruses and hackers taking over your system, they don't just appear out of thin air: some user intervention is required. A virus could come as an email attachment that you download and then try to open, or a bad web-link must be clicked on or an infected system be allowed to connect to your network. As long as you have a reputable Internet security program installed, one that looks for malicious files and stops you opening them, and blocks you from visiting websites that are known to be infected, the chances are that any malicious activity will be spotted and blocked before it can infect your machine. Peer-to-peer technologies like illegal file-sharing software and torrent clients should obviously be avoided – both for security threats and for the fact that the illegal activity can be traced by your Internet service provider to your business if it ever catches up with you. I don't want to bang on about security here, but there are a couple of key steps that you should take so as to have the best chance of sailing the Internet safely.

⎔ *TIP*

Most malware has the potential to completely wipe out your data or render a hard drive inaccessible, so it's really important for you to keep your data backed up regularly – ideally to a location that's not on your internal network.

---

www.avg.com

If you have bought a ready-to-use computer, it most likely came with a trial or cut-down version of a security suite installed – something like Norton or BullGuard – but that doesn't mean that you have to pay the premium subscription when the trial runs out. There are plenty of great free solutions that should be ample to keep most users safe and sound. AVG has long been the most popular and effective free antivirus solution. There is a premium version of the software that you should consider as a small price to pay for more complete peace of mind, but the free version is updated regularly with all the latest protection data and will detect and stop most viruses, threats and malware before they can cause you any real trouble. This service also offers a free, cut-down security app for Android mobiles.

 TIP

countermeasures.trendmicro.eu
Specialist blogs are a fantastic way to keep up on the inside knowledge, with very little effort. Rik Ferguson is a security expert with 15 years' experience (and a really nice guy too!) who writes a regular blog for the online security firm he is a director of. It is well worth checking in frequently with this entertaining and informative blog so as to keep abreast of current security issues.

safego.bitdefender.com

Social media is becoming an increasingly popular target for the spread of malware and viruses, with lots of scam posts being used to spread malicious links throughout your friends' networks. It's never a good idea to click anything on the web that looks out of the ordinary – especially if a post uses language or grammar that you wouldn't normally expect from the person apparently posting it. Safego from Bitdefender offers free protection for your Facebook and Twitter accounts – just authorise the apps and tweak the settings if you want to, then the software will trundle through your accounts, sniffing out all the bad guys, squashing attempted scams before they can spread.

 TIP

It's worth following Safego's Twitter account and checking in with the Facebook page regularly, as they publish links to the latest scams and things to look out for online – giving you and your friends ever more protection against potential fraud.

THE CLOUD DOORMAN

Smart password security tips and tools

A frightening number of security breaches happen because of nothing more sinister than bad password choice. Password security expert Mark Burnett, who blogs on xato.net, has collected and analysed over 6 million password and username combinations over the years and found that a shocking 91% of people have passwords that appear in the top 1,000 most commonly used. A thousand may seem a lot of passwords to try by hand, but a simple program written by a hacker to break into your account could run that many password attempts in a few minutes. He also found that:

- 4.7% of users have the password 'password'
- 8.5% have the passwords 'password' or '123456'
- 9.8% have the passwords 'password', '123456' or '12345678'
- 14% have a password from the top 10 passwords.

Obviously these are not good password choices – any fool can work that out – and yet the temptation to simplify one's own life still makes them an attractive option for the security-unconscious. It's also tempting to use words that are easy to figure out by looking at your personal information – such as pet names and family birth dates. Social media has made this kind of information easier than ever for people to discover, so you are better off avoiding any words or number combinations that might be connected with your life. A secure password should use capital letters, numbers and special characters to make it harder to guess, and should be changed on a regular basis. If you want to be super-secure there are several good online solutions for managing your many passwords.

lastpass.com

LastPass is a password manager that lets you create incredibly secure and very unmemorable passwords for all of your website logins, with only one central master password to remember. There are versions covering various operating systems, browsers and mobile configurations, and although some do require a premium account at just $12 a year it's not a lot to pay for total peace of mind. The free LastPass account covers all mainstream browsers and operating systems and can be accessed online through their website, so should be plenty for most users. Once it's installed you still need to go through all your accounts and shore up security – changing passwords to something less obvious than password123 and making sure that you use a different one on every site.

www.yubico.com

For those who want to be über-safe, there's a relatively inexpensive hardware option at Yubico. The USB YubiKey works with LastPass, among other password manager services, and it means that no one can access your accounts if they don't have the physical key to plug in. That does mean you too, however, so make sure that you keep it somewhere safe, like on your key ring.

TIP

www.grc.com/securitynow.htm
Another great place to keep up with the latest security threats is the Security Now! podcast with online celebs Leo Laporte and Steve Gibson; a security guru who coined the term 'spyware' and wrote the first anti-spyware program. The podcast is published weekly, free, and will ensure you know exactly what to look out for and the best ways to protect yourself.

www.vitamindinc.com

Intruders don't always come at your computer through your broadband connection, especially if you work in a shared office space. Vitamin D is a neat little application that turns an inexpensive webcam into a proximity-aware security camera, kicking in to record video footage any time someone approaches or moves unexpectedly around your desk. It may not stop them from attempting to break in to your machine, but at least you will know who it was. It's really quick and easy to set up and you can even instruct it to send an email alert when activity is detected. The single-camera Starter Edition is free to download and use; a couple of premium versions are available for multiple cameras and with more features.

www.lookout.com

With mobile Internet becoming more integral to our daily lives, I want to remind you about a service that we looked at back in Chapter 5. If you haven't installed Lookout (or similar) by now, what are you waiting for? As well as making regular virus sweeps, it will automatically back up all your phone's data online so that you can easily reinstate it to a new handset should the need arise. One hapless thief was caught out by this when he took photos of himself on his newly 'liberated' Android phone, only to find that the backup process had provided its genuine owner with a handy mug shot to give to the police! I know I've already mentioned it, but it really is a no-brainer to protect your mobile.

PERFECT PRESENTATIONS

Impressive alternatives to making boring PowerPoint presentation slides

Ever found yourself nodding off at the back of a conference hall? Your audience can find even the most informative presentation like wading through treacle if you're not careful. Masterful use of transitions and keeping the number of words to a minimum can help, and personally I get bored looking at slide after slide of bullet-pointed lists – there are many more imaginative ways to present a list of facts to a live audience, and I want to share a couple of presentation-building applications now that will really unlock your creative potential. I want to be up front too, and tell you that these packages will take a bit of learning how to use, especially if you have no real experience with graphics or design software. It's worth persevering, though, if you want to make dynamic and exciting presentations and promotional films and to deliver memorable pitches. I do a fair bit of public speaking, and whether the audience is made up of a handful of company executives or a school hall full of GCSE students, people always ask me afterwards what I used to make the presentation. You can push through the early learning curve by having a look at some of the pre-made templates and seeing what you can do to them, before working up to creating your own designs.

> ## TIP
>
> *If someone asks what software you used to make your presentation (because they will!), use it as an opportunity to swap contact details with them by offering to email the link if they give you a business card.*

prezi.com

Prezi is an old favourite of mine that is fun to use and delivers really stunning results. With a few clicks you'll be building a cascading, zoomy mind-map (yes, that is the official technical term) – although be careful not to get carried away with the effects and end up making your audience feel a bit seasick. You can drop in slides containing text, images, video, graphics and even bullet-pointed lists if you really want them – then set the path for your presentation and watch it fly. The free account lets you create Prezis that are open to the public; if you want privacy and a vanity web address for sharing, you'll have to pay the subscription, or if you work in education you can apply for a full subscription free of charge.

 TIP

kuvva.com
A change is as good as a rest, they say, and with Kuvva installed on your desktop machine (PC or Mac downloads available) you will find a new, beautiful piece of art or photography installed as your desktop wallpaper when you boot up every day.

www.powtoon.com

PowToon is another great fun application that produces both animated slide shows and short films in a number of very current design styles. There is a limited (though still generous) choice of templates and character sets with the free account – with premium options for more (of course). This is quite a complex piece of software, so again, begin with one of the demo films and start clicking on the items in the timeline and exploring what menus and options come up. There are tutorials in the help sections of both of these packages, so never be too proud to read the manual. With a little patience you'll soon be recording your own voice track (using Audacity from Chapter 3 – do you see a pattern forming here?) and having your words animate on and off screen, with all sorts of characters and props to interact with. It's a great way to launch an eye-catching and memorable promotional campaign. The end result can be uploaded straight to YouTube, or downloaded and shared in a number of other ways. The free account limits you to 20 YouTube uploads a month with a lower-resolution film of only

45 seconds maximum (at the time of writing, though this can all be subject to change as the company finds its feet following launch). The pro upgrades look a little expensive until you consider the quality of what you can make and how much it would cost you to commission an agency to produce anything similar.

TIP

ninite.com
Take the pain out of keeping your software up to date by getting Ninite to do it for you. With only one click from you, the app runs all over the web to collect the latest updates for all of your nominated software and add-ons, which is a lot less time consuming and laborious than doing everything by hand. The premium service lets you install an auto-updater so that your computer stays up to date by itself.

 Profile

Emma Jones, Founder of Enterprisenation.com

"It's never been so cheap to start a business, so we're seeing real innovation in young start-ups. This is why large corporates, government and the crowd are saying we will extend those small amounts of funding to help people get started."

Emma Jones started her first business at the turn of the millennium, encouraged by the dot.com boom and operating out of the spare bedroom of her Manchester apartment to help inward investors move to the UK. Just 15 months later the company was sold to a big PLC and Emma turned her attention to setting up Enterprise Nation, an online community, training and events company aimed at supporting and encouraging home business start-ups. She is one of the eight co-founders of StartUp Britain, which we looked at in Chapter 3, and in June 2012 was awarded an MBE for her services to UK enterprise. As well as having a busy campaigning schedule and speaking engagements across the world, Emma is a prolific author, having written a number of best-selling books around the subject of starting and growing a successful business from home. Her next book, due out around the same time as *Working the Cloud* in early 2013, tackles one of the issues she sees raised often within the home business community registered at Enterprise Nation: exploring ways you can grow your business from home without outgrowing your home office space.

Emma said:

When I started Enterprise Nation I really wanted to help people who had done what I did: set up a company from home. I started Techlocate in the spare bedroom of my apartment and when we sold the company two years later we were still just five members of staff working out of home offices in London and Manchester. I remember renting a meeting room in serviced offices when we met the purchasing company's financial director to discuss the value of the company, and we put family photos on the side to make it feel like this was our regular office space. In the end we needn't have worried as the finance director said that one of the reasons they wanted to acquire us was because we had kept overheads so low and based the business from home. The thing to understand about the Internet in its purest and most simple sense is just how powerful it is for any small business owner. I was amazed the other day when I saw a figure saying 40% of small businesses are still not online. When you consider the power of the Internet and how it enables you to source suppliers, find partners and, critically, promote and sell your goods both locally and to a global market, I think that every small business owner should embrace the web. With cloud applications too you can work from anywhere. It really levels the playing field and I think the big multinationals have a challenge on their hands because the innovation and entrepreneurship is all coming from small businesses. This is why it's been fascinating over the past six months to see how many large corporate companies are now starting small business programmes. The crowd-funding trend for business start-ups is also a fantastic option. We've never seen so much innovation in the financial services sector, at a time when the banks are, sadly, not responding to what small businesses need. But the critical thing in the UK at the moment, which is brilliant to behold, is that there are record numbers of people starting a business. One reason is because it's never been so cheap to start a business, so we're seeing real innovation in young start-ups. This is why large corporates, government and the crowd are saying we will extend those small amounts of funding to help people get started.

www.enterprisenation.com

At its heart, Enterprise Nation is a free community website for anyone running a small business, but with a particular focus on articles and features aimed at those running a business in their spare time or from their home. As well as regular features stuffed full of great advice and business resources, there are online and offline events and seminars, start-up loans advice and downloadable kits, question and answer sessions with experts, and of course, Emma's own impressive collection of business advice books and other reading material available in the shop. For many people, working from home can be a lonely experience and the friendly forums and social channels are the perfect tonic for Enterprise Nation members, who each weekday morning at 11am are invited to join in a little social banter with their home-working peers by following the Twitter hashtag #watercoolermoment.

POCKET OFFICE

How to take your essential apps to any computer you work on

If you move around a lot during the working week but can't always guarantee an Internet connection, the cloud is going to be of limited use. Contractors, students and corporate hot-deskers (they are even doing that at the BBC where I work now) will know how frustrating it is to be barred from installing anything on communal computers. You get so used to using those helpful little applications and add-ons at home that you really miss them when they are gone – if only you could carry the cloud around in your pocket. It's funny you should say that.

TIP

If you sign into your Google account in the Chrome browser it will give you the option of using all your settings, password saves and favourites wherever you are surfing the Internet from – including your portable drive.

portableapps.com

PortableApps.com is a useful tool that serves up your choice out of dozens of popular freeware tools that will fit onto and run from almost any device with at least 512MB of space – such as an ordinary USB drive (sometimes referred to as a thumb drive). You can add packages such as OpenOffice, Chrome, Skype, GIMP, Thunderbird email, Audacity and many more apps we've talked about in these pages. Just download the free set-up file (recognised by the extension .exe for 'executable file') and launch it into a wizard that will help you to create your own personal portable drive – make sure that you have a blank USB drive inserted and choose that as the destination when prompted, or whatever external device you want to run it from. You can even install it into a Dropbox folder, though it could be pretty clunky if your connection isn't great. There are loads of apps to choose from, including utilities, office tools, education aids, games and communication software. What you can add will be limited only by the size of the drive on which you're making it. Once it's set up you can just plug in the drive to any machine and run the apps straight off it, with no need for a net connection or local installation.

TIP

Rescue a virus-locked PC by adding the ClamWin antivirus tool to your portable drive, then press the set-up key when the infected computer tries to boot up. Look for an onscreen message – it will be something like DELETE or F8 to enter set-up, depending on your system. In the BOOT ORDER menu you can now ask the computer to launch straight from the external drive, then run the ClamWin tool to clean up any infections.

TIP

Add the VLC Player app to your portable drive, as it is without doubt the most flexible digital media player on the market, being capable of playing without fuss many unusual formats of videos and audio files that other media players reject outright.

SHORT CUTS

Tools for shortening web addresses and short cuts for office tasks

Most articles that you'll want to share will be several pages deep on a website, making the web address far too long for easy posting on social platforms where you're limited on character count per post, such as Twitter. Popular blogs and news sites will have social sharing tools built in, and they will generally have automatic link shortening, which is why you may not instantly recognise the URL you just posted using these buttons. If you want to keep track of the links you share, and even gain some insight into how they are received, you can shorten the links yourself using a dedicated tool. There are loads of these around and they pretty much all let you create custom short URLs and group your links into categories so that you can review them and track sharing activity in order to fine-tune your strategy. These tools are free and many include a browser widget, known as a bookmarklet, that you can drop on your bookmarks bar to shorten a page URL with just one click.

bitly.com

Personally, I like bitly, but that is mostly because I have been using it since the dawn of time (for this type of service anyway) and all of my links and content are saved neatly in its database. Set up an account and link it to your social streams to start tracking your shared links and saving them into 'bundles' that can be shared through a single URL. There's a browser bookmarklet and a Chrome add-on, and even a smartphone app, but only for iPhone currently.

www.longurlplease.com

The flipside to the short URL craze is that it's much easier to hide malicious web addresses behind a generic, shortened URL. With good security software installed your system should catch most harmful URLs before you can open them and unleash the malware on your computer. On the rarest of occasions you may be the 'lucky winner' and find an undiscovered threat for the first time, in which case it's possible your antivirus software won't catch it. As a rule of thumb I never open a web address that comes through Twitter, Facebook, email or whatever if it doesn't come with a message I'd expect to see from the person sending me the link (as we talked about earlier in this chapter, when we covered the basics of security). LongURLPlease.com has a bookmarklet and Firefox add-on that lets you see the root web address of the shortened link you've been given – for example http://bbc.co.uk ..., in which case you know that the source domain is BBC.co.uk and so it isn't likely to contain anything harmful. If lengthening the web address reveals a strange URL that looks completely wrong for what the link is claiming to be, you may want to get in touch with the person who posted it to check that they haven't themselves been infected with a virus – which is how these things generally spread.

qrpal.com

The last shortcut I want to show you uses quick response (QR) codes – which are essentially the modern-day version of barcodes – to make performing basic office tasks as simple as scanning an image with your phone's camera. Once you've set up an account, the service will step you through the process of creating your own QR code for a variety of tasks – including logging onto the building's password-protected WiFi network. You just add the steps and the password to make the connection, and then print out the QR code so anyone who scans it will be connected automatically. I have also used QR Pal to make a QR code that launches my website and have incorporated it into the design of my business card – and because I can control the colour and certain visual aspects of the code it makes a really stylish bit of functionality to add to my first impression. Android and iPhone apps for scanning QR codes and building a database of the content you discover are also free, though it's unlikely most users will have sufficient thirst for QR codes to warrant really using them.

NOT SUCH ODD SODS

Pack up that briefcase and let's move on

I'm sure you'll agree that that was a curious collection of bits and pieces, but no less valuable for their random nature. I could include many more web wonders here but we have to keep pressing on if we want to see you graduate – informally qualified to feel a little bit smug when telling everyone how much time and money you've been saving. Not only that, but your security is now nicely shored up and you should be wowing the pants off anyone who gets caught in the crossfire of your killer presentations. You'd think it's almost time to put your feet up and take a break, wouldn't you? Not so fast, soldier; we have two more chapters to go and they cover topics that are perhaps the most fundamental to really conquering the Internet. We'll start by getting you out to meet people, face to face in the cloud – but without ever leaving your office, of course. Teleconferencing is ridiculously big business online right now, and in the next chapter I'm going to be revealing the worst-kept web secrets that everyone is talking about, and talking on ... And after that? We end with world domination, of course (or at least as close to it as any small business should healthily get).

Chapter 9

I'll meet you in the cloud

The amazing technology that lets you meet face to face in virtual space

---

By now your head is probably reeling with the possibilities of doing business in the cloud, but that doesn't mean you should completely check out of reality. We humans are very visual creatures; in fact it's reckoned that 64% of communication is actually non-verbal, conveyed instead through body language, facial expression and tone of voice. Meeting in person will always be more effective than exchanging a few emails – though perhaps not as efficient – but this doesn't mean you have to clock up hundreds of miles running around the countryside visiting clients and suppliers. There are plenty of ways to enjoy face-to-face meetings online without ever leaving your office, and you don't have to spend a fortune on professional teleconferencing equipment either. This chapter covers the best tools and services for meeting in the cloud – from 2 to 250 people. And, far from being a downgrade, added presentation tools and collaborative workspaces can make virtual meetings feel like an upgrade from their traditional real-world counterparts. In this chapter we'll be taking a wander around the web to look at:

- free and low-cost alternatives to meeting in person
- video-conferencing tools for talking face to face
- group voice calls and teleconferencing with lots of creative tools

- screen sharing from 2 to 250 people
- interview with entrepreneur Paul Gibbons, owner of many golf courses
- online spaces to throw ideas around with distant creative partners
- creative brainstorming and planning tools that you can use together in real time.

CLOUD GATHERING

The best free online meeting rooms

Let's be honest, meetings are a pain in the derrière (usually quite literally, in my experience, as you have to sit for far too long listening to other people's business). They are a necessary evil in any company, but you don't need to burn half the day travelling to and from meetings when you can dial in, just 10 seconds beforehand, over a webcam instead. It's now fairly common for people to hold online meetings with anywhere between 1 and 30 others, much of the time using free video and voice communication that work on the same VoIP technology as we looked at in Chapter 6, where we talked about free alternatives to the telephone. At the other end of the spectrum there are online conferences and 'webinars' (a contraction of 'web' and 'seminars') that seat audiences of thousands without much trouble, even allowing participants to interact through text messages and live chat rooms in some cases. Believe it or not, there are tools to do all of the above (and more) completely free of charge; you just have to know where to look.

CLOUD VISION

Face-to-face video-conferencing tools for two or more

I remember 1970s sci-fi shows depicting space-age video phone calls as being just like watching the telly. How disappointed I was after the turn of the millennium when the experience was still more like watching a slide show of photos taken every few seconds accompanied by some broken-up audio you could just about make out as a voice. We're still not at HD video quality in our homes yet, but we are getting significantly

181

closer as increased connection speeds and improvements in technology are making it possible to fit more and more information into less and less space. Video conferencing is now very much a reality and there are some really high-quality solutions for even the casual user.

TIP

Hangouts is part of the Google Plus social media platform, so can be used on the go through any of the official smartphone or tablet apps for that service. Be aware of data costs when broadcasting video to a Hangout meeting when not on a WiFi connection.

tools.google.com/dlpage/hangoutplugin

Number one on my list of free video-conferencing services has to be Google Plus Hangouts. It goes without saying that integration with Google's other offerings, such as Calendar, YouTube and Google Plus, will make organising and subsequently sharing your meeting (if you want to) very straightforward. All you need is a webcam (you can pick up a perfectly adequate one for £20 – check that it has an in-built microphone) and a Google account and you can meet with up to nine other people, even using the 'On Air' feature to broadcast the meeting live to an audience. A lot of indie YouTube channels are springing up like this, feeding a growing hunger for things like cookery and DIY shows – I even saw one Google Hangout broadcasting live amateur telescope feeds from different parts of the world, accompanied by a lively discussion about astronomy from those broadcasting. This show in particular made use of the screen-sharing feature in Google Hangouts, where you can switch from your webcam to a feed of whatever is on your computer's desktop so people can see a document you're explaining (or a planet you are discussing). Once the meeting is over you can save it directly to YouTube so that anyone who missed the session can catch up in their own time.

TIP

If everyone at the meeting uses Google Docs, you can share and collaborate on the same document, live and in real time. This means that you can all work together and no one has to take copious notes about what was decided because you'll all end up with exactly the same thing on your desktop at the end.

www.teamviewer.com

For more flexibility and the ability to hold much bigger meetings, TeamViewer is a massively popular service with 100 million users in 200 countries. As well as being a professional-looking meeting space with lots of collaboration options, this software gained a lot of traction originally for being a hassle-free remote desktop-connection tool – ideal for troubleshooting PC problems from afar. It's free for private use, with a one-off fee to upgrade to one of the pro versions. These start at more than £400, which seems expensive, but it is all you'll ever pay to use the service. If you do need to hold regular creative meetings for up to 25 people, these packages are so feature rich that I'm sure you won't even blink at the price tag. To run a meeting just share the invite code that you get with any participants and wait for them to join you. There's the option for video, audio, screen and file sharing, plus a whiteboard that overlays your desktop to really help hammer the point home. One really nice touch is that you and your participants don't even need to install the software or have administrator privileges to run the application (very handy in big corporate HQs where the network is locked down for security reasons). Just download the executable file and when it launches choose to run the 'viewer' instead of installing the whole package. You can now start, or join an instant meeting. There are versions for Windows, Mac and Linux as well as mobile apps for Apple and Android.

VOICES IN THE CLOUD

Tools for teleconferences using VoIP

Not everyone has, or even *wants*, a webcam. I know that when I'm working from home most days I would definitely not want to suddenly find myself in a room full of people – but I am happy to sit in my dressing gown and fluffy slippers on a cold morning, attending a meeting from behind the veil of a voice-only call. Apart from reasons of vanity and comfort, not everyone has access to a computer somewhere quiet enough to hold a meeting in the middle of the day – we've all seen them hunched in a quiet corridor listening to their phones. Voice conferencing is also a better choice if you're joining the meeting from a mobile or other slow connection. Video contains at least 15 times more data than audio and so could clog up the line, making it hard to hear anything at all.

TIP

If you're meeting on Skype mobile it provides users with free WiFi across the UK at coffee shops, airports and other public places. You'll need the free Skype WiFi app installed to see if there are any access points near you for free VoIP connections when you're out and about.

www.meetupcall.com

Meetupcall is a conference phone call service that is so simple to use that you may never have another face-to-face meeting again. Just schedule an appointment using something like Outlook, Google Calendar or Gmail, and add Meetupcall's email address to the invitation list. Now the service takes over, keeping everyone informed about the upcoming meeting and who is attending, even compiling and sharing LinkedIn profile details of the attendees so that you all know exactly to whom you're talking on the call. The 'free' account isn't exactly free: there are no sign-up fees but the cost of your conference call is split between a maximum of 20 participants, who all pay around 4.3p a minute to dial in from 10 global locations (which isn't a bad price for a good-quality conference call service, after all). There are subscription accounts for more participants and additional global dial-in locations; the 'pay-as-you-go' option lets you pick up the cost of your participants' phone calls too, if you're feeling generous. Everyone in the meeting is given the choice of a dedicated dial-in number or to have the service call them when it's time to roll – reversing the charges, of course. Once the call is finished there will be a recording available in your inbox if you ever need to check what was said.

TIP

Why burden someone with the responsibility of taking minutes of your meeting when you can just record the whole session and stash it somewhere, either privately or where everyone can check it if they want to remember what was agreed?

SCREEN MEET

Screen casting and remote sharing with small or large groups

We looked at quite a lot of ways to record and share your screen in Chapter 3, but you can also let people dial in live, even listening to you and watching what you're doing as you demonstrate something on your desktop or run a PowerPoint presentation. Google Plus Hangouts and TeamViewer both let you do this very nicely, but if you want to strip out the complication of video and just use a lean, mean, screen-sharing machine, there is plenty of choice (as I'm sure you've come to expect by now).

join.me

JoinMe is a screen-sharing tool that will let you throw one helluva party with up to 250 people invited to share your screen and swap text chat and files. The presenter can also share audio and give over control of the screen to one of the participants. The service describes itself as "ridiculously simple", and it really is. To run a meeting just download and launch the sharing tool, which gives you a JoinMe web address to share with anyone you want to invite. That's it. No registration, and your participants need only enter that URL to be transported to your desktop. If you do register and upgrade to the premium service you'll enjoy more management and scheduling features, the ability to share the presentation delivery with another person, plus the option to share just one window on your desktop rather than your whole machine – quite handy if you want to relinquish control to a viewer but still keep your personal data locked away. As you'd expect, mobile apps for Apple and Android devices round off this offering nicely, as viewers can dial in from wherever they are and have a reasonably high-quality experience.

 TIP

tweet-show.com
If you're running a live event you can let the audience join in using Twitter. Just create a (hopefully unique) hashtag on Tweet Show and run the application somewhere on a monitor or projected into your event space. Now anything tweeted with that hashtag will be displayed on your screen for all to see. Be warned: there is no moderation or profanity filter!

www.twiddla.com

Sometimes you just want to grab five minutes to bash out a creative concept with your business partners; but what if they all live in different cities? Twiddla is a nice alternative to sending a string of boring emails. Just jump on the site and create a channel to which to invite others with the URL you're given. No registration, and you can chat as you play around together in the graphical sandbox. You can even fire up a microphone or webcam if you have them attached, though if you're going to do that I would say maybe head over to Google Plus Hangouts, where the video experience will be much higher quality. The joy of this space is its uncomplicated nature, with just enough creative tools in the box to let your imaginations spark without the spontaneity being sucked out of things by having to wrestle technology.

 TIP

Ever spent 10 minutes composing an email, only to find when you send it that another person in the string has made your comments null and void with their input? Email is too linear for any more than two people to really communicate, so real-time collaboration tools like Twiddla are the way forward.

Profile

Paul Gibbons, Owner of Leaderboard Golf

"The world isn't waiting for you to launch a product. In fact, the world is completely unaware of what you are about to do and they probably don't even care."

Like so many of the prominent business leaders interviewed for this book, Paul Gibbons started work at an early age, joining Burton's retail group when he was just 15. Here he discovered an aptitude for communicating with his customers, talking to them (and their wives) to find out what they were really looking for so he could suggest the perfect garment. He quickly realised that selling would be a key skill to develop and looked for roles that specifically offered high-end training and management development courses. It was during his time with Thomson Regional Newspapers — where he was top sales person for three years running — that he met John Madejski. Together they founded *Auto Trader,* with the first issue (at the time called *Thames Valley Trader*) going on sale in 1977 for just 10 pence a copy. A lot has changed since then, and after selling the iconic classifieds car mag for a reported £260 million in 1998, Paul has gone on to build an impressive portfolio of golf courses and golfing-related businesses. His latest initiative is attempting to disrupt the market for last-minute tee-time bookings, which currently involves big websites taking a significant commission on all bookings. With Leaderboard Golf tee times, Paul wants to offer every golf club in the country a page in its directory for a small monthly subscription, where they can post course information and special offers and golfers can book last-minute tee times directly, allowing the courses to plough more profits back into improving and maintaining their facilities.

Paul said:

I never planned to own the golf course because I didn't want to spoil a good hobby by turning it into a business. But after we sold *Auto Trader* I felt I was too young to retire and when my accountant mentioned the favourable capital gains tax regime on golf investment I decided to set up a business with my wife, Jennifer, and we bought 27-hole Sandford Springs at a 40% discount. If you're thinking of creating a business, priority number one has to be finding out what is available in the way of help from the government in terms of grants and tax breaks. I think the Internet is a great way to start that research, or you could go and speak to your accountant because they should know. The Internet is a developing technology that has really changed every kind of business and you can no longer afford not to embrace it or you'll be left behind. It's much harder to keep up to date with your competition is doing online because the space is so vast, and I'm not sure whether we could have launched *Auto Trader* as a magazine if the Internet had been about in the same way back then. But there is also the big advantage that if you're smart enough and have the right technical people around you (and they're actually not that expensive) you can take on the really big boys in a head-to-head competition – the Internet has made the playing field an awful lot bigger, but it is at least completely level. You can also track the results of your work far more easily, as analytics will tell you which headlines are being clicked and which are not. Someone once said to me: "50% of the money I spend on advertising is wasted. I just wish I knew which 50% it is." This is very true and I think if you spend your money wisely on the Internet you can greatly improve the odds, whereas you really can't when using traditional media. If you're just starting out in business I would urge patience. You have to maintain the drive to succeed, but Rome wasn't built in a day and the world isn't waiting for you to launch a product. In fact, the world is completely unaware of what you are about to do and they probably don't even care. So you need lots of patience and you have to be prepared to educate the market in whatever way you can. Make sure you spend your money well and just believe in yourself and your product.

CREATING SPACE

Places where you can throw ideas around digitally with distant creative partners

Collaboration. It's a word you'll hear a lot when you start spending more time online. The dictionary defines it as teamwork or cooperation. You'll find that the instant and interactive nature of the web makes it the ideal place to experiment. You can open up a space in virtual reality and get together with as many people as you like to throw anything you want into it – text, images, videos, slide shows, bits of code, you name it. Anything from a simple whiteboard with text and basic drawing tools, like we saw with Twiddla a few pages ago, to complex ideas, maps and flow diagrams that you can build and sculpt slowly over time. There are endless ways to collaborate online and I've picked out a few of my favourite free tools for you to start having a play with.

TIP

minecraft.net
To see extreme collaboration in action, take a look at Minecraft, a hugely popular, massively multiplayer game (meaning that lots of independent players can inhabit the same physical space in the game simultaneously) where real people can actually build and shape the environment and everything inside it, one pixelated building block at a time.

celtx.com

Back in Chapter 3 we spoke about making short films to promote your business, or just to entertain your customers online and keep them coming back to your site. If you fancy giving this a go and want to draft in help, celtx is a great collaboration and project-management tool designed specifically for the pre-production phase of media projects like this. Whether you're writing a novel or a screenplay, putting together a short film or comic book, or storyboarding a comedy sketch, there is a tool to help at every stage – even the really boring stuff like project management and location call sheets when you come to set up a shoot. The basic download is free and there are paid subscriptions to get more templates and online storage, plus full collaboration and team work flow management. iPhone users can download the app (either free or paid versions) that lets you storyboard a project on location using your camera phone to take snaps – very handy if you're a budding film-maker.

TIP

www.wreckamovie.com
Have you ever fancied being involved in making a real feature film? Wreckamovie is a community where you can sign up to be part of one of the many exciting projects that members are working on. There are roles ranging from accountancy and graphic design to animators and administrators – all you have to do to apply is sign up and offer your services.

www.authorstream.com

If you want to give a presentation using PowerPoint, you can upload it to authorSTREAM and invite people to join you live as you step through the slides. It's a really professional way to gather a group for a presentation, and if you upgrade to the premium subscription they don't need to register in order to join you. The free account still lets you run a meeting, but it will be ad supported and your guests will have to register with the site to take part. There is also the opportunity for them to download your presentation to refer back to afterwards. This is a great place for sharing and collaborating on PowerPoint presentations, as members are given the option to make uploaded files available for others to download and tweak. Be aware that if you sign up using your Facebook profile the site will vigorously post all your activity and its own daily promotions on your timeline.

TIP

prezi.com
Prezi (the presentation maker we looked at in Chapter 8) also has the built-in option to invite collaborators and viewers to join you online for a live presentation.

TIP

www.slideshare.net
Slideshare, a site we looked at way back in Chapter 1, is based on the principle of being able to share and present PowerPoint slides to anyone you invite to join you on the platform.

TIP

If a group wants to work together on a document, Google Docs has a live, real-time collaboration feature that lets you see changes being made and who is making them – team this feature up with a Google Plus Hangouts meeting if you want to chat about the changes as well.

MIND THE MAP

Mind-mapping and diagram tools that you can use together in real time

Gone are the days when the best way to plan a project was to draw the team's work flow in marker pen on a flipchart; that's too linear when today there are so many elegant and instant ways to plan your work flow interactively on the web. Brainstorming is no longer the domain of pretentious marketing executive-types (although I'm sure there are plenty of them 'thinking outside the box' somewhere online) when using a visual method of planning and mapping out any detailed project can be the most straightforward way of making sure that you don't forget to join any of the dots. This could not be truer than when you are setting up a new business from scratch.

www.mindmeister.com

MindMeister lets your mind wander freely across the possibilities by creating a mind-map of tasks and actions that can grow with nodes and branches from the seed of a brilliant idea. The free account lets you make three maps, and you get up to 10 more if you invite some friends to try the service (with the inevitable premium upgrades for more). Once you've created a map, you can invite collaborators to help you build it, even attaching tasks and deadlines to the nodes so that everyone knows where they stand. There are no frills or complications here – it's just a beautifully simple mind-mapping tool that lets you focus on executing the idea or business plan rather than on the logistics of keeping track of it all.

creately.com

The mind-map is just one type of creative template, and at Creately you can bash your craniums together using one of more than 40 types of creative tools, including flow charts, wireframes, process flows and mind-maps – whichever suits you best – and there are thousands of pre-made project templates to give you a headstart on common types of task. You can invite up to 20 collaborators working together in real time, as the diagram updates live on everyone's screens. The free account gives you limited diagrams and projects and only three collaborators, but it's certainly enough to see if it's worth an upgrade for you. Even used for planning the odd project without a team, this tool is an absolute gem for keeping things organised.

 TIP

If you decide to buy the desktop version of Creately you will still be able to work on your projects if your Internet connection goes down (although obviously real-time collaboration won't be possible). Any changes you make to the diagram will be synced to your online files when your connection comes back online.

bubbl.us

If you want to experience the ultimate in simplified creativity you can step back in time to the most basic brainstorming tool at bubbl.us. This website has tooled down the mind-mapping process to the point of almost being patronising. "Start Brainstorming" screams a big fat button on the opening page, inviting you to click through and then follow the two-step prompts to making the embryo of your ideas chart – and that's really all there is: two steps. Click to create a new node and click to write something in it. If you're feeling adventurous you can move the nodes around on the page to group them by dragging with your mouse pointer – just point, click and hold, then drag. You don't have to be a professional planner to save time by using these kinds of tools, so next time you reach for a marker pen and flipchart, maybe flip open your laptop and head to one of these sites instead.

ALTOGETHER CLOUD

You came, you saw, you drank lots of tea and probably argued a bit too

If you're anything like me, one meeting a week is more than enough – perhaps I shouldn't have burdened you with so many ways to join in. You can cut down on the fluff by making sure that you plan and adhere to a detailed agenda, assigning everyone their time to speak and locking them down to a topic ahead of time so that the meeting can't get derailed by issues no one has researched yet. Maybe it's a reflection of the rapid-fire communication streams we're becoming used to online, but I've found that people on a video or conference call tend to get to the point a lot quicker than in real life, and with the whiteboard tools and other display bells and whistles I've shown you in this chapter. understanding each other should be a lot easier too. If all else fails, you can keep half an ear on the conversation and get on with something more useful at your desk (which I think is another good reason to avoid video conferencing, if I'm being totally honest). All this should add up to spending much less time banging your heads together without getting anywhere fast. So, we're nearly at the end of our journey and I really hope you've freed up lots of time by using the cunning tips and tools in this book, because I have a feeling you're about to get busy again. I have just one thing left to ask you before we wave goodbye to Chapter 9:

Are you ready to make some money now?

Chapter 10

Cash clouds

Easy ways to make extra money out of
time spent online

Before you get too excited, this chapter isn't going to turn you into the
next dot.com millionaire; not on its own anyway. We will be talking
a little about e-commerce and setting up your own online shop, but
this isn't about jacking in your nine-to-five and harvesting fifty-pound
notes from the Internet full time. Instead we'll be exploring the ways in
which you can start bringing in a trickle of income to supplement your
cash flow just by following the steps in this book so far – particularly if
you're creating content or making a serious attempt to build and engage
a following on your website or social media pages. We'll be taking a
wander through the virtual souks where you can sell your photographs,
digital creations and even real-world arts, crafts, belongings and stock
(whatever that may be) with little or no start-up cost beyond whatever
inventory you choose to hold. Aside from e-commerce and advertising
there are plenty of other risk-free ways to make money online and I'll be
revealing the best throughout this chapter. From paying guests in your
home or camping in your garden to getting 'the crowd' to invest in your
£1 million idea, we'll leave no cash-generating stone unturned, including:

- earning money from advertising revenue
- making money from YouTube videos
- online markets to sell digital art and photography
- becoming a citizen journalist for cash
- online auctions and selling actual stuff
- independent e-commerce websites

- the crowd-funding phenomenon
- interview with Jean Oelwang, CEO of Virgin Unite and Sir Richard Branson's right-hand woman
- the new 'global village' economy and how to use it
- turning the spaces you own into cash in the bank by renting them out to others.

MONEY FOR OLD CLOUD

Earning advertising revenue for work you're probably already doing

Five years ago you'd be hard pushed to find a blogger with as much influence as they have today – and that's basically down to social media. With so many people connected across the world, a story (good or bad) can spread like a virus (hence the term 'going viral'), and that's a valuable commodity in this web-connected world. When people visit your website or watch the video you posted on YouTube, you could be earning money, just like the company that hosts the content – all you need to do is add some *ads*. The mainstream services that we'll be looking at next have all made it pretty easy for you to set up and start monetising the time you spend creating content by including advertising messages in your pages. This barely scratches the surface of what is out there, so consider this a starter's guide to the world of online ad revenue that you can tap into.

 TIP

AdSense allows you three banner ads, three link ads and two search boxes per page. Think carefully about the best place to put the search boxes – perhaps where visitors might want to look for more information, like at the checkout rather than where the eye first lands on a page.

AdSense on accounts.google.com

Throughout this book we've spoken about the dominant nature of some of the online giants, and it was never truer than of Google when it comes to advertising. AdSense is arguably the only advertising revenue platform you'll ever need – and because, like everything in Google's stable, it is free and pitched at being adopted by the not-so-techy masses, it's actually relatively simple to set up and start earning. Log in to your account page and you'll find the link to set up AdSense in the 'Products' menu. There will be an authorisation process with html code to add to the web address that you want to monetise – very similar to when you were setting up Analytics back in Chapter 3. Completing registration gives Google permission to place adverts on your website that are targeted at key words identified within the content – so in theory they will be ads for stuff that your visitors might want to see. You get to control the aesthetic detail, like size, colour and placement of the banners, and this is really important as you get paid only when somebody actually clicks the AdSense banner. Getting the placement and style right is an art form in its own right, but you have to be careful in your quest for clicks as there have also been some issues in the past with smaller accounts being banned for various (usually hotly contested) reasons. If you decide to go with AdSense, here are my top tips for keeping your nose squeaky clean and still making some money.

- Place banners at the top centre of the page, as it will be the first thing that comes up onscreen as the images load, and your visitor's eye will naturally be drawn there while they wait. Don't make banners so big that you lose more readers than you get clicks, though – experiment with size, colour and placement until you find a set-up that is tuned to engage your audience.
- Read the terms of the service carefully – which I know you won't, so to paraphrase the key bits, if you don't want to get shut down by Google for trying to cheat the system: you are not allowed to (a) click your own ad links, or (b) ask others to click them for you, however subtle your request is. Google is all about spotting patterns in data, and you won't get away with trying to game the system. You just won't, even if you didn't mean to.
- Different key words have different values attached to them, depending on demand from advertisers. You can rearrange the placement of ads within your banners to make sure that the words with the highest value are in the most prominent places on your page.

- If you had the bright idea of looking up AdSense's 20 most valuable key words and building a site purely around that, I really wouldn't bother. With terms like 'insurance', 'treatment', 'loans' and 'attorney' it's going to be tough work building an audience of any meaningful size in those areas unless you are a genuine expert. You might get the odd stray hit, but you'd be better off providing a real service and earning dozens of clicks at a much lower rate in the long run.

- Ultimately, it's a numbers game. You can't make people click your banners, and I wouldn't advise even trying. On average you can expect 2–3% of visitors to click the banners (known as a 'click-thru rate'), so the more people you can attract to your website the more money you are going to earn.

 TIP

Don't place too many ad banners right at the top of your page or Google will penalise your website's page rank, reducing your potential audience. Stick to no more than two banners above the fold so as to maximise earnings without reducing visibility.

 TIP

wordpress.org/extend/plugins/easy-adsense-lite
Many popular blogging platforms and website builders will have pre-made plug-ins and extensions for managing your AdSense banners more easily – like this one for WordPress bloggers.

MOVIE MONEY

Monetising your YouTube videos with in-built advertising

You may not think it's worth adding advertisements to your YouTube posts, but you never know what will catch the imagination of the crowd and go viral – and since it costs nothing to set up you don't really have a lot to lose. There is a pretty famous clip called 'Charlie bit my finger' in which a young lad gets his finger bitten by his teething baby brother. That 57-second clip has been viewed almost half a billion times, reportedly netting the family more than $150,000 – and it will continue to earn them cash as more people click to watch it. I'm not saying that you can expect that level of success, but who knows? As you saw in Chapter 1 in the case of Seth Casteel, if it happens, it generally happens fast and you have a limited time to cash in. As well as this, there is a growing number of independent content makers earning regular six-figure sums on YouTube. There's absolutely no reason why you shouldn't also bring in a few bucks for your hard work and creativity (or lucky captures on film, as is more likely to be the case).

Monetising www.youtube.com

When you open up your video manager dashboard you'll see a banner inviting you to click and start monetising your account. Once cleared, you can choose to include adverts on your video posts, clicking every time to confirm that you own all the rights before deciding which types of ad to include.

www.ebuzzing.co.uk

Another way to make money online is to write articles or create videos to support a particular 'sponsored' campaign. This might mean that a brand actually pays you to make content around a specific topic that its customers will be attracted to; or you might just get a free piece of kit if you promise to publish a fair appraisal of it. This is completely ethical as long as you make it clear to your readers what they are getting – and you don't let the contribution cloud your editorial judgement. Ebuzzing is a platform that connects you with advertisers who are looking to run this type of campaign. Your registration will have to be approved by the team – it needs to recruit people who have a decent-sized audience to see the adverts, after all – and then you can make your skills available to thousands of brands around the world that are signed up to spend advertising budgets through the service. Non-VAT-registered users should sign up as 'other' rather than as a professional organisation.

TIP

Ebuzzing Labs is a section of the site that tracks what's going viral and being watched on websites like Facebook, so even if you don't want to become a campaign publisher it can be a good place to look for inspiration if you're thinking about making your own video series.

CASHING IN ON CREATIVITY

Selling photographs, artwork and other digital creations through online markets

The first known banknote was produced in China in the 14th century: the 'Great Ming Circulating Treasure Certificate'. A simple act of faith allowed a value to be attributed to what was effectively just a piece of paper – and the entire modern banking system has been built on this principle. I guess that the point of the story is to illustrate that anything has a value if someone is willing to pay for it. Just create a piece of art or take a stunning photograph and you may find someone out in the ether who finds it valuable enough to want to part with their own cash in order to possess it – or at least to possess a copy of it printed on a coffee mug or T-shirt. The digital economy in the UK is worth £121 billion a year and, as you'd expect, there is a growing number of ways to connect with potential customers if you want a slice of this e-commerce action.

www.deviantart.com

DeviantART is the world's largest community of artists and art lovers, where more than 2 million people a day come to explore and exhibit their work, both for kudos and for cash, as there is the option to sell your best work through the print shop, transforming things like T-shirts, cups and canvases. It's free to set up a profile and build your gallery, with a commission payable on any sales that you make. The social features means that once you catch the public's attention there is a good chance that more browsers will be attracted to you, leading to potentially greater sales. Have a browse through what's there to see the huge range of styles and formats displayed on the site – you never know, it might even spark something profitable in your own imagination.

Check out the site's tutorials in order to refine your skills in things like graphics, animation and image effects. You will be improving your skills as well as improving your chances of making something somebody wants to buy.

www.scribd.com

If you think that your writing might be worth something there is a site that we looked at way back in Chapter 1 that could bring in a little profit. Scribd's store lets you showcase your work to the site's 100 million plus members. That doesn't mean that they are all in the market for buying your words, but with membership numbers like this you have the best chance of finding an audience. From stories to recipes, academic reports or poetry, it's a completely risk-free way to put your toe in the water of the professional writing game.

CITIZEN JOURNALISM

Selling photographs and videos of the world you see around you

Filmed by an 'eye witness', clips recorded on smartphones and other mobile devices are finding their way onto the six o'clock news more and more often, in a trend that's been dubbed 'citizen journalism'. If you happen to be in the right place at the right time to capture something newsworthy there are agencies that you can sign up with that will pay you decent cash for those images – professional photographer or not. But as well as those 'right place, right time' moments, there are other agencies looking for 'stock images' to include in their catalogues. These images may be licensed by other content makers for use in their own work, in which case you'll get a (usually quite small) payment known as a royalty for your trouble. If you fancy having a go at making some cash from your camera, I've lined up a selection of places where you can jump on board for free to see if you get any bites – but be aware that your work will be among hundreds of thousands of others' vying for attention on these platforms, so don't go picking out your chrome-painted Bentley just yet.

TIP

Demotix recently upped its breaking news game with the release of an app (iPhone right now, with Android to follow soon) that lets you capture and send breaking news photographs as the story is unfolding.

www.demotix.com

Budding photo-journalists can register with Demotix in the hope of selling their stories to various international news outlets. This site is all about breaking news, so it's not really the place to sell artistic shots of your grandma's country cottage – though it won't cost you anything but time if you want to try. When you register you'll get an email explaining how to upload a story. The website acts as an agency, selecting the best images uploaded on the day and putting them in front of the picture editors at all the top news organisations around the world. Unless you've captured a very unique and newsworthy moment, your images will need to be quite high resolution to make the cut, as we are talking about professional publications. There is even a possibility of your story being picked up as an exclusive, netting you a significantly higher fee (which will be negotiated by and split with Demotix, of course).

TIP

You'll get a lot more out of this site if you are actively in the kinds of places where 'news' happens. Take a leaf out of the paparazzi's book, and if you see a crowd gathering outside a branch of your local record shop wander over with your camera to see what's going on.

www.shutterstock.com

If you still think that the photograph of your grandma's cottage is worth something then you should head over to a site like Shutterstock. It boasts over 20 million stock photos, images, graphics and videos – which on the one hand is good because there will be plenty of customers browsing the archives, but on the other hand means that your work will have to find a way to rise above all that noise if you're going to make any money. It will accept all manner of high-quality photos, from animals and architecture to food, drink and yes, even the odd kitten, which might then be picked up and licensed for use in things like commercial websites, brochures and advertising campaigns.

www.scoopshot.com

A more casual service can be found at Scoopshot. This is a free 'snap and sell' iPhone app that lets you make a little extra money on the fly with your mobile camera. You set your own price and terms when you upload an image, so make sure that you have a good idea of what it might be worth. One feature I really like is the client-request broadcast, which sends a notification to any app users in a particular location with a request for something specific from a customer. For example, a designer in Scotland might want a photo of the Thames from a particular angle for a brochure about investing: they send the request out through Scoopshot and if you get back with the right photo before anyone else you can make some money out of a small licensing deal. Just like that. Any profits you make are shared with the Scoopshot service.

 TIP

hashpix.com
Instagram aficionados with a decent-sized following of active fans could turn their interest into income with the help of Hashpix. Not all registrations are accepted by the network but applicants who are accepted will be given a dedicated web address from which to sell high-resolution prints of their photographic work to followers and fans.

foap.com

Another free iPhone app that lets you sell snaps is Foap. Here there is a set price tag of $10 per shot — just register and start uploading images that you're happy to sell, and you split any income generated 50/50 with Foap. You can also check out the mission pages where buyers have posted requests for particular types of images. Although at the time of writing Foap is available on iPhone only, its website states that an Android version will be released soon, so check the Play Store or join me on WorkingTheCloud.biz to find out more when you pick up this book.

TIP

www.tunecore.com
Budding musicians might make their lucky break with the help of TuneCore. This is a digital distributor that claims to get your music on sale across all the mainstream services including Spotify and iTunes for the price of a pizza and a six-pack.

www.huntzz.com

For something completely different why not turn your hand to making a smartphone app that can be sold for real cash in an open marketplace? Sounds a little out of your reach? Think again and download Huntzz on your iPhone or Android. This free app lets you make a treasure hunt in the real world based on GPS markers, snapping photos and writing clues as you record the trail for others to follow. If you live close to a historic location and have some detailed local knowledge you could make fun and educational tours, advertising the app through your social network to get people to download it. Think of it as being like creating an interactive book. You never know, you could discover a hidden talent and spend the rest of your days hiding virtual treasure.

TIP

You don't have to charge for the treasure hunts you publish and this would be a great way to run a fun promotional campaign to engage local customers. Just set a time limit for people to complete a local-knowledge hunt in return for whatever discount voucher or special offer you have placed at the end of the trail. Don't forget to post the details on your social networks and encourage people to join in.

SELLING THE REAL STUFF

Online auction sites and marketplace outlets where you can sell actual stuff

E-commerce is booming – it's actually one of the fastest-growing markets in Europe right now, yet is still overlooked by many as a genuine way to make an income. We spent more than £50 billion online in the UK in 2011, and, as I write, forecasters expect a 14% increase in 2012. When you consider how every other market seems to be contracting right now, that's a pretty healthy growth rate. The rise of open auction sites and the online equivalent of market stalls has played a large part in the public's growing acceptance of e-commerce, making it so quick and easy to get your listings online that you can often have a new shop up and running in under an hour. The founding father of the online auction site has to be eBay – a business started in 1995 that now has around 2 million people browsing listed items every day. That's an awfully big potential audience, and if you can find something that they want to buy, you could be quids in with no initial set-up fees and very low running costs.

TIP

If you don't mind getting up super-early, and have an eye for a bargain, you could join the legions of people making decent money cherry-picking the best items at car boot sales and bric-a-brac fairs to sell on eBay. Be careful not to get carried away and end up for months with a spare room full of junk, though.

www.ebay.com

eBay isn't just about offloading your bric-a-brac and unwanted wedding gifts (although it works just fine for those purposes too, if you like). Almost £750-worth of goods changes hands across the site every second. Shoppers go there because it's quick and convenient to buy stuff, and you can find listings for pretty much anything you could imagine – from the utterly mundane to the truly bizarre. I've seen listings for a papier-mâché urinal (wouldn't want to be in the room when that was used!) and even someone selling his mother (or at least photos so you can pretend that she's your mum). Canny traders can do good business just by going to the 'inconvenient' places to buy stuff cheaply before marking it up and selling it on through eBay. Once you have registered, you will see that it's very straightforward to list an item. Make sure that you take care in producing your posts – a decent photo and a good description are essential to making the best sale. You can use the image-editing and online-hosting tools mentioned back in Chapter 4 to help you. Tips and advice for running a successful eBay shop full time would make a book in their own right, and there is plenty of reading on the subject online if you care to Google for it. I would definitely advise taking a look at the many auction-management and automation plug-ins and services that are available if you decide to take eBay trading seriously.

 TIP

www.gopesa.org
An independent trade body called the Professional eBay Sellers Alliance, or PeSA, has been set up to support those merchants who want to formally turn their eBay trading into a full-time business.

 TIP

A study by the Journal of Consumer Research *found that red backgrounds lead to more aggressive bidding, so photograph items on a red background if you can, in order to subliminally encourage better sales.*

www.etsy.com

Now, you can sell pretty much anything on eBay — although it recently banned listings for existential and made-up stuff, like ghosts in jars and love spells. But if you've got something more hand-made and crafty (in the non-devious sense) to offer, Etsy is the place where all the cool kids hang out. This is the best-known open marketplace for artistic types to display their wares, and gaining popularity on the site comes served with a good dollop of digital street cred. Etsy was started in 2005 by a group of people who just wanted an easy way to sell their own creative endeavours; it grew rapidly and now the website's blurb declares the lofty goal of wanting to "empower people to change the way the global economy works". From hand-made jewellery to vintage clothing and way, way beyond, there is something for everyone's taste here. You don't have to be a professional artist to set up shop on Etsy — in fact only about a quarter of sellers are — you just need a niche, artsy product at a reasonable price and some of the 42 million unique visitors a month are likely to buy one.

TIP

www.collectplus.co.uk
If you own a corner shop or convenience store anywhere in the UK
you could join a network of over 5,000 small businesses that take in
parcels for local customers of online retail giants like Amazon and ASOS.
Don't expect to earn a fortune from the Collect+ scheme directly, but
one major retail chain claims to have seen a 20% rate in 'collateral'
purchases while the collector is in the store picking up the parcel.

SERIOUS E-COMMERCE

Setting up shop through an independent website

Like so many other UK traders, you may decide to set up (online) shop on your own. To do this you will need a website that supports online transactions, a feature that may cost you, depending on your supplier, but that a lot of the better-known website-building tools will allow you to do. In fact we looked at some back in Chapter 3, as you may remember. Weebly is currently the best e-commerce choice from that selection, as there is no limit on the number of listings or bandwidth and currently it does not charge commission on transactions. You'll also need to register with a secure transactions service to take online payments for you; and it will need you to have a merchant account into which it can pay your funds. PayPal is a very common choice but there are other options; your own bank may well offer the service if you ask it. I would advise researching costs at the time of setting up shop, as this is the kind of market that is now moving rapidly. If that all sounds a little complicated, to be honest it probably is. That's not to say that you won't be able to figure it out with the help of our old friend Google and a little persistence. There are much easier ways to achieve a similar effect, though.

www.shopify.com

For dipping your toe in the water of serious e-commerce, Shopify provides a safe haven to pitch your stall and see if any customers take an interest. You'll get a dedicated URL towards which to point customers, which you can customise with themes and design tweaks before loading up your (virtual) shelves with all your products. There is a free 14-day trial, after which monthly payments start at £19. The extra outlay will buy you more storage space and product listings, or SKUs – which is short for 'stock keeping units', and so denotes the number of separate product strands you can offer simultaneously. Also, note that unless you go for the most costly account option there is a small percentage fee for handling transactions, on top of the monthly subscription.

TIP

www.transactsocially.com
Instead of giving stuff away free during a promotion, sell it for some social publicity. Transact Socially puts a button on your web pages on which your customers can click to automatically promote your message on their Facebook and Twitter streams in return for whatever promotion you're running.

THE CROWD FUNDING PHENOMENON

How bright business ideas can become reality with the help of mass online investment

For most of you the ideas we've thrown about so far are going to sit nicely alongside an existing career or business commitments. Spending just a few hours of your time each week without any financial risk is a great way to try out any new idea. But what if your ambitions are much grander (or at least more immediate) than that? If you've tried borrowing money from a bank recently you'll probably have a fair understanding of what people mean when they refer to the 'credit crunch'. But as it becomes harder to secure investment from financial institutions, an interesting innovation is taking root in the social web. Crowd funding broadly means securing investment for a project from lots of individual backers, typically using a campaign driven on the social web. Kickstarter was the first of these platforms to really get things moving back in 2009 – although donation websites for charity projects, which is a very similar business model, have been around for some time longer. Beginning in the USA and now firmly entrenched in UK culture too, at first it was more about funding established art forms. Literary and short film projects were very common, bringing coffee table books on obscure topics to life or making an art-house director's vision of a dystopian future a reality by asking the very niche potential audience to fund production with what effectively amounts to advance orders. I've clicked the big button to back a couple of those projects myself in the past and have always felt that I got value for money (although not always a timely delivery!). But in recent months there has been a definite shift towards gadgets and gizmos as well, with projects like the Bluetooth 'Pebble watch', which displays information and apps from your smartphone, attracting more than $10 million worth of backers against a target of just $100,000. Next came the incredible success of a computer game called Double Fine Adventure, which raised $1 million in less than 24 hours. These outstanding performances are being repeated often enough for local government to start taking an interest (if the Kickstarter blog is anything to go by, at least). As crowd funding shifts from being thought of as an extended 'art grant' and into something far more important to global economics, I think we can expect to hear much more about it in the future.

TIP

If you're going to seriously attempt to get crowd funding you need to approach it like a marketing campaign. The social aspect is what makes this platform so effective at getting projects of all kinds off the ground, as the most popular projects are naturally promoted to other would-be investors. If you post your idea and just sit there waiting for investors to come to you, you're likely to have a very lonely wait.

www.kickstarter.com

I'm not here to help you come up with a killer idea, so let's assume that you have this part of the Kickstarter journey already sorted out. There have been some real stinkers of ideas put forward in the past – like the book titled *Crowdfunding: A guide to what works and why* that failed to get out of the blocks on Kickstarter – so make sure that your idea isn't among them. Registering and setting up your project page is all pretty straightforward but there is definitely an art to making your campaign successful. If you want to know more, that's a journey you'll have to take on your own from here, as the topic is another book in its own right (I'm going to be busy, aren't I?). You will find plenty of great reading online though, if you search for something like 'how to run a successful Kickstarter campaign'.

 TIP

Research has shown that for an average $10,000 Kickstarter project you have a slightly better chance of achieving your goal if you set the funding duration to 30 days (35%) rather than 60 days (29%). The same study also found a direct correlation between number of Facebook friends and your chances of success.

www.indiegogo.com

Far from it being the only crowd funding platform in town, the million-dollar success of so many Kickstarter projects has encouraged impressive growth across this sector and there is plenty of competition blooming. Indiegogo is one popular service that competes well with Kickstarter, if you want to shop around.

www.crowdcube.com

Similar success stories are beginning to be seen through sites like Crowdcube, which is another choice for crowd funding in the UK. Check the terms of all the new services before making a big decision such as where to host your campaign, as you may find a much better deal than those available today. Don't forget that you can always join me at WorkingTheCloud.biz if you want to find out and discuss the latest news in this area.

 TIP

www.gambitious.com
Gambitious is a crowd funding platform targeted specifically at the gaming sector. In this new crowd funding model, fans can donate money to any game project, the same as with Kickstarter. Outside the USA, though, investors can exchange cash for an equity stake in a project. This twist could see small indie games companies raise significant sums in future, which is good news for die-hard games fans and the market as a whole.

Profile

Jean Oelwang, CEO of Virgin Unite

"As we move more rapidly to a 'global village', crowd funding and other social media tools are turning our notion of community upside down and allowing us to bring good ideas to scale much more rapidly."

Jean Oelwang is often referred to as Sir Richard Branson's right-hand woman. Starting out in the telecoms sector, she travelled the world to help set up mobile phone companies in emerging markets before deciding to walk away from the corporate world to volunteer for VISTA, which is a bit like the domestic Peace Corps in the USA. She landed in a homeless centre for teenagers in Chicago and it was there, she told me, that she realised "how broken our siloed government, business and social sector systems were as I watched young people as young as 12 try to survive in the streets". These memories stayed with her as she went back into the world of business and then ended up joining the Virgin Group to help set up a mobile phone company in Australia in the late 1990s. Four years on she decided to pursue her dream of trying to change the way the business, social and government sectors work together, and as Sir Richard Branson was also looking to start up a foundation for the Virgin Group at that time she put a plan together, pitched the idea to him and Virgin Unite was born. Today the organisation's aim is to help incubate new approaches to global leadership, driving change and building a wonderful community of people who never accept the unacceptable and who believe that business can and must be a force for positive change in the world.

Jean said:
The most important thing for small businesses to realise is that their brand is owned by people all over the world. Social media

has democratised power. Small businesses (actually all-sized businesses) need to truly embrace and understand the power of listening that the Internet offers, which will transform the way they build their businesses. I love the idea of crowd funding, as it furthers the notion of community and really leverages the wonderful digital tools that are now available. As we move more rapidly to a 'global village', crowd funding and other social media tools are turning our notion of community upside down and allowing us to bring good ideas to scale much more rapidly. In this new era of radical transparency, brands and companies are no longer owned by marketing and central management teams; they are owned by people. Companies who want to thrive need to embrace this new paradigm and start treating customers as part of their community rather than just as numbers in a spreadsheet. Crowd funding takes this one step further and allows people to have financial ownership as well. I would say you don't need to climb the corporate ladder and get involved in the dreariness of politics to run a successful business; if you constantly do what you think is the right thing to make other people's lives better, success will come. And do what you love. Don't compromise, and stay on a path that is true to your dreams. So many times people, especially females, fear taking a career diversion to do something different. These twists and turns are often the turning points in your life that give you a much wider perspective on your purpose. For example, when I left the corporate sector to become a VISTA volunteer, everyone made me feel as if I was stepping off a cliff and that I could never get back on the corporate ladder. That year radically changed my life and paved the way to my current role – and was one of the best years of my life!

www.virginunite.com

At the centre of Virgin Unite's mission is the aim to unite all of the global communities attached to the vast Virgin brand and use their collective entrepreneurial spirit and considerable corporate resources to drive change in the way people do business, putting people and the planet at the core, alongside profit. The website publishes lots of inspirational stories and information about events and initiatives it is running, but there are tips and practical advice for businesses of all sizes too. Imagine what a different world we would live in if every business thought about what is best for people and the planet in everything it did. On the website you'll find eight steps for transformation to help guide your own business in making a difference in the world. It has also gathered hundreds of stories to inspire you of businesses that are doing great stuff following this ethical business ethos.

SOCIAL TRADE

Trading directly from person to person in the new 'global village' economy

Freelance workers make up around 5–6% of the entire UK workforce right now and that figure is growing steadily. As one of those freelancers, I can tell you that there is nothing more fulfilling than being able to pick and choose the jobs you do, but equally there is nothing more stressful than looking at a blank spell in your calendar with no new work on the horizon. These tough economic times have meant more unemployment, but could also be seen as an opportunity, as companies are forced to reduce employment liabilities and fulfil some jobs using contract workers. I don't suppose you'll be surprised at what I am going to tell you next (having already heard it dozens of times throughout this book): the web provides the perfect platform to connect with potential employers for temporary and contract work. Here are a couple of interesting new platforms to start you along that path.

www.peopleperhour.com

Sometimes a job is only a couple of hours long and buyers want a quick way to connect to someone with the right skill set for a one-off contract. As a freelancer you can post your availability free at PeoplePerHour, a simple networking platform that lets you advertise your abilities and how much it will cost to hire you per hour, and also lets you browse any listed jobs. The service is quite new, but critical mass is building fast and, with social functions such as recommendations and reviews, the community should strengthen even more over time. There is no charge for 'buyers' apart from reimbursements of any credit card fees incurred during payment. If you're selling there is a percentage commission on your paid hours – all clearly described in the FAQs.

TIP

Buyers should consider using the 'escrow payment' feature that allows them to place the fee for a job in a holding account with the website until such time as the work, or any milestones agreed with the seller, has been completed satisfactorily.

sooqini.com

Another very new service that connects people with time to spare for random short-term engagements is Sooqini. This network caught the attention of the UK press around the time of the Olympics in London, as people were trading for things like "queue at an Olympic event for me and I'll pay you £30". Other common odd jobs include waiting in for a parcel delivery or putting together flat-packed furniture. You can also use the service to sell anything from books and allotment vegetables to tutoring services and accountancy. It's quick and easy to sign up and start advertising, with a small commission on any transactions completed through the site (currently 15% on PayPal transactions). If you prefer, you can arrange to trade in cash, in which case there is no charge by Sooqini (although, obviously, take care about with whom and where you arrange this kind of transaction). The addition of an iPhone app (with hopefully other formats to come soon) makes it possible for sellers and buyers to have their posts broadcast to a geographical location in order to make the perfect connections.

TIP

If you are approaching retirement age and finding it hard to contemplate a work-free life, this kind of network can help you to keep up a trickle of income with limited hours per week, using the skills you've spent a lifetime perfecting.

flattr.com

If you're providing a service on your website that people find useful you could try asking them to donate a small payment to help you with your running costs. You see this quite often on the pages of shareware downloads: "it's free but if you fancy bunging us a few quid we would be very grateful" kind of thing. Flattr is an interesting idea that makes this process super-easy by letting users set a monthly balance, say £5, that gets split between any websites they choose to Flattr during the month – in other words to 'thank with a donation'. For you as a business it costs nothing to add a Flattr button to your site, and takes only a few minutes if you know how to add a snippet of HTML code (something we've done several times already in the chapters of this book). You're not likely to earn much, as the concept hasn't really exploded yet, but it is gaining a decent following as time goes on. And every little helps – right?

THE SHARING ECONOMY

Turning the spaces you own into cash in the bank by renting them out to others

Some call it 'collaborative consumption', to others it is the 'sharing economy' or even 'peer-to-peer rental'. Whatever moniker you choose, it boils down to the same basic principle of renting something you own directly to somebody who needs it, without going through a middle man. This could be a spare room in your house, or a spot in your garden where holidaymakers can pitch a tent and explore the surrounding area. There are even networks growing that let you share the cost of running a car or rent out an unused parking space. One of the barriers to growth in this market is establishing trust, but some leading platforms are beginning to make enough money out of this business model to put significant insurance policies in place to ensure that every party is protected. Couple this with the fact that more people seem to be coming round to a social way of thinking, and the trust objection seems to be fading gradually. With recommendations and customer reviews now becoming more and more meaningful in the decision-making process, there is a real opportunity to join the sharing economy and turn your empty spaces into additional income. Here are a few ideas to get you started.

www.airbnb.co.uk

Low-cost alternatives to traditional holidays are popping up all over the Internet and Airbnb is the latest buzz in peer-to-peer home rental, where you sign up to either rent out or book in to a room in someone's home. Trust is built on the website before booking through ratings and reviews of both guests and hosts, and Airbnb offers the highest insurance policy in the business following some horror stories about damaged properties in the past. Read the terms and conditions to be sure that you know what is and isn't covered in your home. Becoming a host can be a good way to bring in some extra cash occasionally, and you might even make some interesting new friends. For guests looking to book a room, there are listings in over 25,000 cities around the world, and whilst you are not guaranteed 'hotel quality' accommodation – remember these are people's homes you're booking in to – it can make for a cheap and different way to spend a city break.

 TIP

If you're offering a room on a peer-to-peer rental platform in a property that you are renting yourself, make sure that you know your rights with regard to your own landlord, as you might be breaking the terms of your lease.

www.housetrip.com

HouseTrip is another recent start-up in the collaborative consumption market, with a platform very similar to Airbnb where people rent out a room or rooms in their home. With massive investment recently, the platform looks on target to book 3 million nights of accommodation in 2012, becoming a serious contender in the home rentals market. As this is an emerging trend it's worth taking a look at how these services stack up against each other at the time of reading this, before committing your own home.

campinmygarden.com

At Campinmygarden.com you'll find a community of proud garden owners only too happy to share their space with paying holidaymakers, and you can join them, listing your own place free of charge in the huge directory. Even if you live in the city you may find that someone wants to pay to camp in your garden – just include lots of photos and information about what there is to see and do around you. If you're looking for a cheap and different holiday, it's not just UK gardens featured here: you'll find places to stay in all over the world, as far flung as New Zealand, Indonesia, Mexico and Bolivia. Holidaymakers can search for a place based on the services offered (like toilets, hot water and electric sockets) to discover a very recession-friendly family holiday.

TIP

When setting up your profile remember that you're trying to attract holidaymakers to your garden. Include clear information about transport links and distances from major cities, and have a look on Google or talk to your local tourist board to find out what the best local attractions are.

gocarshare.com

If you're planning a road trip and have spare seats in the car, why not do the environmentally friendly thing and see if you can fill them with paying trade? It could be a one-off trip to a festival or cross-country, or perhaps you commute regularly and want to share the burden of the rising price of fuel and running a car. Advertise your journey on goCarShare to recruit someone to share the costs – which, according to the site's 'Questions' section, should not affect your insurance as long as you're not doing it purely for profit. It's completely free to connect with other members, as all payments are handled directly between yourself and whomever you take on the journey. The obvious caveats about meeting with strangers from the Internet apply, so make sure that you stay safe and smart.

www.parkatmyhouse.com/uk

If you live in a busy town or city where parking is restricted, it can be quite expensive for those travelling to the area to pay for a council- or privately run car park. You can turn an unused parking allocation into a trickle of income by advertising the space on a service like ParkatmyHouse. It's free for anyone looking to hire a space and it just takes five minutes to register and get set up through the website or free smartphone app. For 'sellers' it's free to list your space but there is a 15% fee on any successful transactions. Check your own landlord's contract for potential conflicts if you're leasing the space yourself.

HANDBRAKE ON

Gearstick into neutral, kill the engine, listen to it tick

It seems somehow fitting that this journey should end at a parking space, somewhere safe and familiar where you know you can rest for a while after what has probably been quite a long and dusty road trip. I hope you've enjoyed the 'sites' along the way (do you see what I did there – sights, sites?) and I'm aware that I have crammed my personal, decade-long journey into just a few weeks of reading for you (assuming, of course, you didn't buy this book 10 years ago and are only just finishing up reading it, in which case it must seem like a dinosaur). This final leg of our journey has probably been the most challenging, as it takes a leap of faith to start letting the Internet have any real influence over your finances, especially if you come from a generation that didn't grow up with this kind of technology as second nature. The media love to talk about a drama, so you are bound to have heard plenty of terrible stories about people being ripped off and scammed online. It does happen, yes, but it's not that hard to stay safe and there are genuine opportunities to make money, as I hope I've demonstrated throughout this chapter. Whether it's targeted advertising revenue, flogging off unwanted stuff or seed funding for a new business plan, there are plenty of risk-free and completely legitimate ways in which you can turn a profit online.

Final word: see you in the cloud

The bit where you get to explore on your own

It may be time for us to finish travelling together, but in truth your journey has only just begun. The tools and tips laid out in these chapters should give you a solid-enough foundation to build on, but it will take time and effort on your part to really make them pay off. If you're serious about your business it won't feel like hard work, as with every step that you take down the road towards mastering the Internet you'll find things will work better, get easier or start making more money. I hope that you manage to find a network or two that really fit – it's definitely worth persevering, even if you don't think you need one. As several of my interviews have pointed out, running your own business can be a lonely experience. Technology has given us ways to grow and to share our lives like never before, and sometimes you need to just take that leap of faith to see how it can make your life easier. If you choose to continue on your own from this point, I wish you luck, and I know that you won't regret it. I can't come with you but you'll find me at WorkingTheCloud.biz if you want to call in occasionally to pick up new maps and get your windscreen cleaned; or, if you just want to ask me to lay off the cheesy car analogies, to be fair, everyone is welcome. If you have an Android or Apple smartphone or tablet you can also download the free companion app, which launches with the full interviews with my wonderful contributors in text, audio or video formats. In the future I will be releasing additional content on this app – such as interviews, reviews, how-to guides and other special articles – as text, audio or video features. I hope that these chapters have been able to inform and inspire you to start staking your own rightful claim on the web. You don't have to do everything all at once – though I am available online with oxygen and sympathy if that's the route you decide to take – but try to do *something* at least. You could be surprised by where you end up.

Glossary

Algorithm   The dictionary defines this as "a step-by-step procedure for calculations". In the context of this book where I have referred to an algorithm it means the steps that a search engine goes through to deliver the best answers to a query, or similar web-service programming.

App   Short for application, this usually refers to a self-contained smartphone- or web-based application.

B2B   Business-to-business transactions or trades.

Browser   The software interface that you use to explore the Internet. Chrome, Firefox, Opera, Internet Explorer and Safari are all very popular examples.

Collaboration   In the context of this book it usually refers to working together with other web users on some group, usually creative, project.

Crowd fund   To gain investment for a business idea or other goal from a large group of people connected to you via the Internet.

Crowd source   The same as crowd funding, only with the goal being to collect information or knowledge or to carry out some other collective goal.

E-commerce   Buying and selling things online.

Embed code   A snippet of software code that you can add to a web page to open a window to the content that you want to share on it.

GPS	Global Positioning System – exactly like your car's satnav, smartphones and tablets have a GPS system that software developers use to make location-aware apps.
HTML	HyperText Markup Language – this is the basic language for building the web. You don't need to know it or understand it to enjoy your time online, but you may hear it referred to when customising your web experience – such as with embed codes, which are made up of HTML.
ISP	Internet service provider – the company that you pay for your connection to the Internet.
Key word	A word that reflects the nature of your search query or the content of a written article, for example.
Link	A word or words on a web page that, when clicked on, will take you to another web page. Links will often appear underlined in the text and will change colour once you have clicked on them.
Location-aware	An app or piece of software that knows where you are geographically and uses that information to enhance your experience of using it.
Malware	Malicious software that can be introduced onto your system in many ways, but will be protected against with an effective, up-to-date firewall and antivirus software.
Open source	A software coding movement that is built on the ethos of providing software that others can download free of charge or change to suit their own needs.
OS	Operating system – the core software that allows you to use the hardware that you call a computer or smartphone.
Page rank	How interesting your page appears to search providers, based on a lot of variables such as the websites that are pointing to and from yours, and the key words in your text.
Peer-to-peer	Transferring data directly from one Internet user to another, without going through a third party or saving it elsewhere on the web to be downloaded later.

Plug-in (or add-on)	A small piece of software that when added to a larger software program alters it in some way – such as adding extra features or changing the way that it looks.
SEO	Search engine optimisation – the art of increasing your page rank so that the pages you are offering appear higher up the list of links returned to a search query.
Smartphone	A mobile phone that connects to the Internet and makes use of modern apps to deliver an enhanced experience.
Social media	The platforms built to help connect people through the Internet, for business or pleasure.
Spam	Unrequested email or other electronic communication that is used either to advertise products and services or to spread malicious software.
The cloud	Wikipedia says: "Cloud computing is the use of computing resources (hardware and software) that are delivered as a service over a network (typically the Internet)." Technological purists would say that 'the cloud' refers to a specific network over which certain services are delivered, usually specially built for the purpose. I'd like to broaden that term a little to include the Internet as a whole. After all, it was in effect the first 'cloud' ever made – a network built to distribute data – and so everything that exists within it sits in the mother of all clouds, if you like. So, for the purposes of this book, when I refer to 'the cloud' I broadly mean 'doing stuff on the Internet' as opposed to downloading it to your computer to do when you are not connected to the Internet.
Troll	Someone who posts comments on social media sites and web pages that are designed purely to elicit a negative reaction.
URL	Uniform resource locator – this is to a web page what your postal address is to you: the place where it can be found on the World Wide Web.

Virus	A piece of software written to infect, disable or in some way adversely affect the operation of your computer.
VoIP	Voice over Internet Protocol – the software technology that allows you to make a voice call over the Internet instead of over the telephone network.
WiFi	Wireless fidelity – the combination of hardware and software technology that allows you to transfer data from one device to another without the need to connect them with physical wires. This can be information in packets of data over a local network, or connecting you to the wider world of the World Wide Web through an internet service provider (ISP).

Sources

All web addresses quoted here were live at the time of writing, however these are subject to change.

INTRODUCTION

kpinternetmarketing.com/internet-statistics-for-2012
www.ericsson.com/campaign/opportunitysupportsystems/
newsfeed/posts/15-heading-towards-50-billion-connections
www.growthbusiness.co.uk/news-and-market-deals/business-
news/2116438/business-creation-rebounds-after-thousands-lost-to-
recession.thtml
mashable.com/2012/03/20/internet-percent-us-economy
searchengineland.com/study-72-of-consumers-trust-online-reviews-
as-much-as-personal-recommendations-114152)
www.thedrum.com/news/2012/06/19/small-british-businesses-not-
keeping-technology) European Commission's Digital Agenda
www.hmrc.gov.uk/budget2012/sme-4756.pdf
www.futureagenda.org/pg/cx/view#305
www.bitrebels.com/social/internet-habits-then-now

CHAPTER 1

thesocialskinny.com/99-new-social-media-stats-for-2012
blog.hubspot.com/blog/tabid/6307/bid/30030/LinkedIn-277-More-Effective-for-Lead-Generation-Than-Facebook-Twitter-New-Data.aspx
mediatapper.com/google-plus-facts-and-figures
www.tecmark.co.uk/google-plus-stats-2012
mashable.com/2012/08/02/higher-google-search-results
www.huffingtonpost.com/2012/02/14/underwater-dog-photos-seth-casteel_n_1277404.html
www.hmrc.gov.uk/budget2012/sme-4756.pdf

CHAPTER 2

en.wikipedia.org/wiki/List_of_virtual_communities_with_more_than_100_million_users
www.ebizmba.com/articles/social-networking-websites
www.sec.gov/Archives/edgar/data/1326801/000119312512325997/d371464d10q.htm
www.planetsoho.com/blog/2012/07/theres-no-such-thing-as-free-publicity-facebooks-promoted-post-feature
online.wsj.com/community/groups/small-talk/topics/you-use-facebooks-promoted-post
mashable.com/2012/03/09/social-media-demographics
afterhours.e-strategy.com/twitter-demographics-2012-table
mashable.com/2012/08/02/higher-google-search-results
thesocialskinny.com/99-new-social-media-stats-for-2012
blog.conduit.com/2012/05/03/9-facts-picked-up-from-internet-world-2012

CHAPTER 3

www.business2community.com/blogging/blogging-statistics-facts-and-figures-in-2012-infographic-0238960
www.slideshare.net/James_TDP/16-web-user-behavior-statistics-you-should-know-online-user-behaviour-analysis
www.makeuseof.com/tech-fun/interesting-facts-about-the-blogosphere

CHAPTER 4

www.worldwidewebsize.com
mobithinking.com/mobile-marketing-tools/latest-mobile-stats/
e#lotsofapps
scoop.intel.com/what-happens-in-an-internet-minute
blog.backblaze.com/category/backup-news

CHAPTER 5

www.marketingprofs.com/charts/2012/7584/email-content-still-
most-likely-to-influence-buying-decisions
mashable.com/2012/07/31/email-overload-tips
www.radicati.com/?page_id=46
dolphin-browser.com/2012/03/12-mobile-factoids-for-2012-did-you-
know-that
www.forbes.com/sites/markfidelman/2012/05/02/the-latest-
infographics-mobile-business-statistics-for-2012
thesocialskinny.com/99-new-social-media-stats-for-2012

CHAPTER 6

www.enterprisenation.com/blog/the-rise-and-rise-of-cappuccino-
commerce
www.mediapost.com/publications/article/146033
www.themarketingblog.co.uk/2012/03/uk-spends-292-million-on-
daily-deals-in-just-six-months/?replytocom=6311
www.sipnology.com/company/20-voip
www.computerweekly.com/news/2240162166/Smartphones-to-
replace-landlines-within-five-years?asrc=EM_EDA_18544021

CHAPTER 7

mashable.com/2012/07/31/email-overload-tips
www.email-marketing-reports.com/metrics/email-statistics.htm
mashable.com/2012/08/01/email-workers-time

www.bgr.com/2012/08/28/spam-revenue-200-million-cost-estimates
techcrunch.com/2012/07/15/evernote-libin-interview

CHAPTER 8

xato.net/passwords/more-top-worst-passwords/#more-269

CHAPTER 10

www.dailymail.co.uk/femail/article-2068938/Charlie-bit-finger-The-boys-100k-57-second-YouTube-video.html
www.retailresearch.org/onlineretailing.php
lifeinc.today.com/_news/2012/07/24/12906708-when-ebay-bidders-see-red-bids-rise?lite
www.kickstarter.com/help/stats
www.appsblogger.com/behind-kickstarter-crowdfunding-stats
www.kickstarter.com/blog/the-year-of-the-game
www.companybug.co.uk/how-many-freelancers-are-there-in-the-uk

Acknowledgements

In the time-honoured tradition of writing a book, there are a few people I would like to thank because they have made the whole thing possible. They have shared knowledge and insight, listened patiently, commented wisely and course-corrected when I occasionally drifted off track. They have supported and connected me, kept me going and in some cases reminded me when it was time to stop. Thank you all, I couldn't have done it without you.

My incredible interviewees: Seth, Theo, Henry, Duncan, Rajeeb, Tony, Martin, Doug, Emma, Paul and Jean, all inspirational and very busy people who took the time to share their thoughts with us.

All the fantastic publicity people who made those interviews happen. Hilary for writing the Foreword and Benjamin for making that happen. Alan for keeping me technically grounded. My brothers for being my 'open source' minders. Twitter for being 'the minder' of everything else and always being ready with a good answer if I can't find one myself. Jon and everyone at Crimson for believing in me and going along with so many of my hare-brained schemes. Aurasma for the beyond-awesome chance to make an augmented reality book cover and Neil for connecting us. The Faber & Faber Sales team who I know are going to do an awesome job. The makers and developers of all the wonderful websites and apps featured in these pages – as, let's face it, without them you would be holding a notepad.

And you, for buying this book – or at least picking it up in the bookshop and reading this page, which makes me look popular even if it doesn't earn me any royalties.